High Definition Postproduction:
Editing and Delivering HD Video

DATE	ISSUED TO

High Definition Postproduction: Editing and Delivering HD Video

Steven E. Browne

ELSEVIER

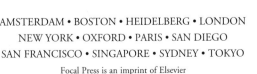

AMSTERDAM • BOSTON • HEIDELBERG • LONDON
NEW YORK • OXFORD • PARIS • SAN DIEGO
SAN FRANCISCO • SINGAPORE • SYDNEY • TOKYO

Focal Press is an imprint of Elsevier

Focal Press

Senior Acquisitions Editor: Elinor Actipis
Assistant Editor: Robin Weston
Marketing Manager: Christine Degon Veroulis
Senior Project Manager: Brandy Lilly
Cover Designer: Eric DeCicco

Focal Press is an imprint of Elsevier
30 Corporate Drive, Suite 400, Burlington, MA 01803, USA
Linacre House, Jordan Hill, Oxford OX2 8DP, UK

 Recognizing the importance of preserving what has been written, Elsevier prints its books on
acid-free paper whenever possible.

Library of Congress Cataloging-in-Publication Data
Application submitted

British Library Cataloguing-in-Publication Data
A catalogue record for this book is available from the British Library.

ISBN-13: 978-0-240-80839-0
ISBN-10: 0-240-80839-8

For information on all Focal Press publications
visit our Web site at www.books.elsevier.com

Printed in the United States of America
06 07 08 09 10 11   10 9 8 7 6 5 4 3 2 1

Working together to grow
libraries in developing countries

www.elsevier.com | www.bookaid.org | www.sabre.org

ELSEVIER   BOOK AID International   Sabre Foundation

For the hours of understanding, patience, and support…

In other words, for all the help and love, I would like to dedicate this book to my life companion and wife, Michele, without whom this book would not exist.

Contents

Acknowledgments

Nothing of value is ever easy, especially putting together a book. No matter how short or long it is, there are people who provide support, information, and expertise to help create the text. It is these people I would like to thank for all their help with this book.

Thanks go to Mark Coan, Brittaney Parbs, Mark Rodrigues, and Paul Apel from New Wave Entertainment. I would also like to extend my appreciation to Elinor Actipis, Betsy Harrell, and Robin Weston from Focal Press.

Also, a thank you goes to Dane Cook, Brian Volk-Weiss, Vito J. Giambalvo, Breht Gardner, and Toby Wilkins for their help with the real-life examples of high definition programs.

And a very special thank you to Graeme Natress, whose thoughts and comments were priceless.

Introduction

When I first saw a high definition (HD) image, I was amazed. The picture was vibrant and filled with tremendous detail. After buying my own "HD ready" high definition television with a separate tuner, I was even more impressed that I could watch this stunning broadcast in my home. I could see individual faces in a football crowd. The raindrops during a live baseball game looked like real rain, not blurry streaks that got in my way.

It wasn't long before I was dealing with the details of high definition postproduction. I quickly learned that it might be easy to watch a high definition broadcast, but it is another matter altogether to actually dive into the complex and confusing high def postproduction landscape.

While standard definition NTSC certainly had created its own challenges, HD posed those challenges and more. Just trying to understand the differences among 12 HD broadcast formats, along with the increasing number of production formats, was confusing to say the least.

Several new HD cameras have since arrived on the market, and with the advent of optical disk and solid state media recording, videotape, at least as a production medium, may well be on its way to the junkyard already populated by 8 tracks, VHS, and corded phones.

But despite the confusion and many production and postproduction choices, it is obvious that the long-awaited move to HD production has begun. Even cable producers have recognized the need to produce their shows on HD, if for nothing else to protect the content for future DVD and ancillary sales.

The first thing I learned in my first few discussions of high definition was this: although high definition has been around for quite a few years, it wasn't being used very much. With little demand, high cost, and few programs, there simply was no interest to migrate to a new, confusing medium.

Now with the advent of HDV and affordable new HD cameras on the market, HD is taking off.

Broadcast networks, cable programmers, and prosumers have been instrumental in encouraging HD productions. And now, even the general consumer has become aware of high definition—even if they're not totally sure what it is. With the federal government mandating television manufacturers to include high definition tuners in sets, the acceptance of and interest in HD has increased tremendously. Add to that the exciting advances in nonlinear editors, HDV cameras, playback decks, and tapeless recording cameras, it's clear that HD is here to stay.

Still, HD postproduction is not easy to understand. Even though there are only 12 high def *broadcast* formats, there are *over 50 production formats,* and the list is growing rapidly. Hopefully, some of these production formats will eventually be retired; in reality, some of these formats are "bridging formats" needed to transition from NTSC-compatible formats to digital-only broadcasting. However, others will remain and more are sure to be introduced.

One thing is certain: careful preproduction planning will continue to be extremely important, especially in the HD postproduction workflow.

Another fascinating aspect of the high def world is that HD—and even, in some situations, HDV—is being used for productions intended to be projected on film. And the use of HD for film is not just for the small budget production. Major motion picture studios have already used HD as a primary production medium. The prospect of a digital pipeline from the set and location, through postproduction, and even into the theater is already here.

High definition can be the best thing since color broadcasting, or it can turn into a nightmare of format conversions, confusion, lost effects, and hours of stress. We will take a look at this HD maze—how others are successfully doing it, and how it is transforming the television, industrial, and film production environments.

The two main goals of this book are to clear up many of the misunderstandings that have evolved around high definition technologies, and to clarify how this family of formats integrates with each other and our familiar NTSC, standard definition video.

I still remember that first day, looking at a high definition image and being amazed. Now it appears that clarity will become the norm.

CHAPTER 1
High Definition—
A Multi-Format Video

"High definition" refers to a family of high quality video image and sound formats that has recently become very popular both in the broadcasting community and the consumer market. High definition (HD) in the United States was initially defined as any video format that had more than 720 (horizontal) lines of vertical resolution. The ATSC (Advanced Television Systems Committee) created a digital television (DTV) broadcast table that defined not only the vertical resolution but also other aspects of the HD frame rate and size. This table defined two sizes of high definition images: 720 (horizontal) by 1280 (vertical) lines and 1080 (horizontal) by 1920 (vertical) lines of resolution. Along with the two frame sizes, there is also a choice of frame rates: 23.98, 24, 29.97, 30, 59.94, and 60 frames per second.

Why This Book Exists

Just looking at the previous paragraph, it is apparent that there are quite a few format choices in HD. To add to the confusion, there is an issue of manufacturers and even professionals mislabeling technical formats and processes. My goal is to identify the misinformation issues and generally describe what is happening in the HD world, giving the reader a basic understanding of what high definition is and what its possibilities are in the near future.

The main purpose of this book is to explain the choices that HD offers and to point to some of the current "accepted" production

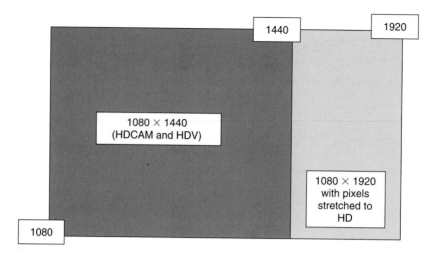

Figure 1.1 Several camcorders do not record the full 1920 lines of resolution when storing 1080 format. Instead, 1440 lines are recorded, and then on play out the horizontal pixels are stretched by 33%.

paths that are being used today. Incredibly, there is still a great deal of confusion even in the professional world concerning HD. There are a few established workpaths—certainly with daily broadcasts of HD programming on cable and OTA (over the air) broadcasting this has to be true. Yet a lack of understanding or just a lack of communication has created costly mistakes that show up in the postproduction phase.

This book should, at the very least, clear up some of the misconceptions and point to the easy path from production to delivery.

Also known as "HD" and "high def," high definition video has rapidly become a consumer buzz word. After years of languishing in the shadows of the popular and totally accepted standard definition (NTSC) format, high definition has finally taken the step into the spotlight. With exciting, low cost, and high quality HDV cameras, new camera lines coming along with even more rapid developments in editing and video displays, consumers

Table 1.1 The HD ATSC Broadcast Table.

Format Level	Vertical Pixels	Horizontal Pixels	Aspect Ratio	Scan Mode	Frame Rate
HD	1080	1920	16:9	Progressive	24 or 23.98
HD	1080	1920	16:9	Progressive	30 or 29.97
HD	1080	1920	16:9	Interlaced	30 or 29.97
HD	720	1280	16:9	Progressive	24 or 23.98
HD	720	1280	16:9	Progressive	30 or 29.97
HD	720	1280	16:9	Progressive	60 or 59.94

The HD ATSC broadcast table shown displays the 12 high definition broadcast formats, six of which are designed to integrate with the NTSC broadcast frame rate. When the analog NTSC broadcasting frequencies are returned to the federal government in February of 2009, the integer frame rates will probably be used more often. Many professionals think there are only six high definition digital broadcast formats, but these are the NTSC compatible frame rates. The others are integer frame rates either used for true film transfer or for future integer frame rates. Note that the only interlaced format is the 1080 frame size.

and professionals alike are diving into HD with money, interest, and passion.

HD has gone from obscurity to being a household term. High def flatscreens have become a "must have" technological "cool item" like the iPod and cell phone. HD has left the esoteric video world and plunged headlong into the mainstream. High definition video televisions, cameras, and recording devices are now being embraced by retailers, beleaguered broadcasters, excited independent film-makers, and even reticent movie studios. Even more exciting is the extremely rapid pace at which improvements are being made in the manufacturing of production equipment, editing, and effects, and probably most importantly for continued growth, consumer products are getting better and cheaper.

Rather than being a single record and playback format, the high definition family offers a matrix of choices that include frame rates, frame sizes, and compression processes. Along with these obvious differences noted in the ATSC digital television table, there are many other production choices in high definition.

These options of what format to shoot and deliver are usually decided by the network or the broadcast company long before production commences so that the postproduction workflow runs smoothly. Students, independent filmmakers, and documentary producers are choosing alternative workflow paths. These creative individuals are pioneering new ground and techniques, some of which have been embraced, while others have been left behind as unsuccessful.

High Definition is Settling Down and Growing Up

When one first realizes the great number of production format choices that currently exist, making the decision as to the correct one for your project can seem overwhelming. But there are some consolations. There are several production formats that have become established as standards.

High Definition Size

In the broadcasting world, most professionals refer to HD as video that is compatible with the 12 standards as defined by the ATSC DTV broadcasting table. As mentioned earlier, the ATSC DTV table cites two frame sizes for high definition: 720 (vertical) by 1280 (horizontal) lines and 1080 (vertical) by 1920 (horizontal). However, there are several video recording processes that record 1440 horizontal lines of resolution in a horizontally reduced ratio. Then, when it is played out, the horizontal pixels are stretched by 33% to produce 1920 lines of resolution (HDCAM and HDV) (see Figure 1.1).

Delivery Determines Production Format

When considering a production's acquisition format, one has to examine the delivery aspect of the program to determine how the high definition image will be recorded.

The particular aspects that should be considered are the following:

- Frame size—either 1080 or 720 vertical lines of resolution

- Frame rate—23.98, 24, 29.97, 30, 59.94 or 60 frames per second

- Bit depth—usually eight bits but sometimes 10

- Compression—a variety of types exist, the most common of which is chroma subsampling

At this time, there are over 60 production and manufacturer choices in the high definition family, and more are on the way.

History

The HD choices began when the ATSC created the digital television table of 36 digital broadcast (DTV) formats. Of those 36 formats, 12 are high definition. These are the formats that the United States government has determined will be the standard for digital broadcasting.

Just as there are many compatible production formats developed for NTSC broadcast, the 12 high definition formats also have a number of compatible production formats to choose from. However, where NTSC has a single frame rate and a single frame size, the DTV high definition format has a dozen different choices. As a result, there are even more possibilities when it comes to the hardware that captures and records those images.

Also, as technology improved, each NTSC production format was basically compatible with the next. However, in the high definition world, not all the frame rates are compatible with each other.

The net result is that there is often confusion about which format should be used.

A Typical Family

In reality, high definition is not a single format at all, but a family of broadcast and production formats with a variety of choices on the set, in postproduction, and even for broadcasters.

- There are three elements that are usually indicated in a high definition notation: frame size, recording method, and image rate. Because this format is new to many people, the order of these aspects is not standardized, and there are verbal shortcuts.
- For the purpose of consistency, this book will notate HD in the following pattern:
- Frame size, recording method, and image rate. So a 1080 frame size shot progressive segmented at 29.97 would be notated as the following:
- 1080psf29.97
- However, a 1080 interlaced at 29.97 is usually notated as 1080i59.94

The reason for this is that the interlaced 29.97 format has 59.94 images per second, and this notation sets it dramatically apart from the progressive frame rate. It could also be notated as 1080i29.97, but one can see the potential for confusion. It can also be called 1080i, 29.97i, and 1080i59.94.

For the purpose of this text, interlaced 1080 will be noted as 1080i59.94.

Because not all the high definition frame rates are compatible with each other, preproduction planning is vital to the success of any high definition project, much more than for a standard definition project.

Ideally, the delivery frame size and frame rate should be established well before any production begins. This allows for testing of specific cameras, editing equipment, and even effects. There are so many new developments occurring in the HD equipment world, one should always check to see what the current workflow, equipment, and other devices are that have become accepted into the HD community.

Some formats can only be digitized or edited on specific editing systems. Shooting at an incompatible or different frame rate and/or frame size from the final delivery format can potentially cause

Figure 1.2 Sanyo HD1. Sanyo's HD1—a low cost consumer HD camera that shoots progressive 720 frames, uses MPEG4 compression, and can take 5 mega pixel stills. Many videographers are purchasing HDV cameras even if their end product is going to be in standard definition because the higher quality of HDV is apparent even when down converted. (Photo courtesy of the Sanyo Corporation.)

costly delays and expensive problems during the postproduction process.

It is important to note that although HD can be recorded in specific frame rates and sizes, different cameras have different "looks." HDV and HD cameras can record their high definition images at various data rates by employing different types of compression. Again, because there are so many production choices beyond the 12 DTV broadcast formats, care must be taken when planning an HD production.

The "Universal" Format

One high definition frame rate, 1080p23.98, is able to be converted to many other high def frame rates and sizes. As a result, this format is informally called a universal format. As an example, if one shoots a program and edits in 1080p23.98 and outputs the resulting program in the same format, the edited master can be converted to almost any format including PAL and standard definition NTSC, often directly from a video playback deck. In many cases, the non-linear editor can also play out the images at other frame rates and sizes.

Although this frame rate has the advantage of being able to convert to other high definition formats, it may not be acceptable as a production format for a particular network. Many networks require that a program be shot *and delivered* in a specific frame rate and size. A rate of 23.98 frames per second has a unique look and may not be the best choice when a production contains a great deal of action or movement. Some clients do not want their camera's original footage shot at 23.98, even though it could then be converted to the specific delivery requirement.

If a company is creating a show for a specific network, sometimes the choice becomes easier. NBC, HDNet, Discovery HD, HBO, and CBS air 1080i59.94. ABC and ESPN air their programs in 720p59.94.

- Progressive segmented frame (PsF) recording is a recording method that stores a progressive image as two separate fields: odd lines, then even. The difference between a PsF frame and an interlaced one is that the two fields of the PsF image are of the same image and then are combined. The interlaced fields contain two separate and distinct images and are not combined but displayed one after another. This, in effect, halves the resolution of the interlaced frame.
- When the PsF image is reconstructed and displayed, it is viewed as a single progressive frame.
- The progressive segmented frame is a technical way of storing a progressive signal using interlace-type technology.

The best solution to any production question is to obtain the company's delivery requirements before shooting begins.

Careful attention needs to be taken when working with high definition delivery specifications. Networks and other broadcasters are very specific about what kind of high definition is being shot, how it is captured in the editing system, and how it is output to tape. Most delivery specs even dictate the length of the slate, where information is placed, and on what lines the VITC (Vertical Interval Time Code) is recorded. Some clients request separate outputs for protection masters, rather than dubs of the original master.

Even More Choices and Confusion

As one can see from the previous high definition tables, there are 12 HD broadcast (as opposed to recording) formats based on frame size, scan mode, and frame rate. Additional confusion about the various formats has been introduced because of the following two issues.

Multiple Labels

The first problem that has compounded the high definition confusion is that individuals, manufacturers, and reporters have used different names for the same technical process or format. Worse yet,

Table 1.2 PAL-Compatible HD Broadcast Formats.

Format Level	Vertical Pixels	Horizontal Pixels	Aspect Ratio	Frame Rate	Scan Mode
HD	1080	1920	16:9	25	Progressive
HD	720	1280	16:9	25	Progressive
HD	720	1280	16:9	50	Progressive
HD	1080	1920	16:9	50	Interlaced

The high definition format is also designed to be compatible with PAL. Because PAL is an integer format, it does not have additional fractional frame rates. The reason PAL runs at a different frame rate is that it was designed for Europe's power structure, which runs at 50 Hz. The United States power is 60 Hz, thus the 30-frame (60-field) and 60-frame progressive rates.

some have used and continue to use the wrong labels. For instance, one individual might call a format 1080i29.97 and someone else will call it 1080i59.94. They are both the same. Another person might erroneously describe the same format as 1080 60i. Rounding frame rates to the nearest whole number can cause problems because six of the HD broadcast formats are whole numbers.

If one is not very precise about a particular format, mistakes can be made. More than one tape has been recorded on location at the wrong frame rate because someone said the show's format was 1080i at 30 frames per second. That tape came back from the location shoot recorded at a true 30 frames per second, when the producer really meant to shoot at 1080i59.94.

Many manufacturers do not use the fractional frame rates for fear of confusing the consumer. Sometimes a frame rate of 30 can really mean 29.97 frames per second, and other times it actually does mean a true 30 frames per second. As a rule, one should only believe a 30 frame per second claim when there is the capability to record 29.97 frames per second as well. Careful examination of a camera or record deck's manual is the only real way to determine if an integer frame rate is really just that. All too often the sales literature, website, and even sales personnel do not really know the exact technical details. Another indicator of what a production frame rate should be is if the program is intended for broadcast. Currently most productions shoot in frame rates that are compatible with NTSC. All NTSC-compatible frame rates are fractional, not whole numbers.

Many Manufacturer Choices

The second confusing issue about high definition production formats is that when color sampling and subsampling, bit depth, compression, codecs, and individual manufacturers' tape and media formats are considered, there are many, many choices. It is difficult to understand what the correct choice really should be.

High Definition is Not New

In 1982, the Advanced Television Systems Committee (ATSC) was formed to establish technical standards for the country's digital

Table 1.3 The ATSC Broadcast Format Chart
The following chart summarizes all 36 ATSC digital television formats (DTV), 12 of which are high definition.

Format Level	Vertical Pixels	Horizon-tal Pixels	Pixel Shape	Aspect Ratio	Scan Mode	Frame Rate*
HD	1080	1920	Square	16:9	Progressive	24/23.98
HD	1080	1920	Square	16:9	Progressive	30/29.97
HD	1080	1920	Square	16:9	Interlaced	30/29.97
HD	720	1280	Square	16:9	Progressive	24/23.98
HD	720	1280	Square	16:9	Progressive	30/29.97
HD	720	1280	Square	16:9	Progressive	60/59.94
ED	480	704	Rectangular	16:9	Progressive	24/23.98
ED	480	704	Rectangular	16:9	Progressive	30/29.97
ED	480	704	Rectangular	16:9	Progressive	60/59.94
ED	480	704	Rectangular	4:3	Progressive	24/23.98
ED	480	704	Rectangular	4:3	Progressive	30/23.98
ED	480	704	Rectangular	4:3	Progressive	60/59.94
ED	480	704	Square	4:3	Progressive	24/23.98
ED	480	640	Square	4:3	Progressive	30/27.97
ED	480	640	Square	4:3	Progressive	60/59.94
SD	480	704	Rectangular	16:9	Interlaced	30/29.97
SD	480	704	Rectangular	4:3	Interlaced	30/29.97
SD	480	640	Square	4:3	Interlaced	30/29.97

This digital broadcasting chart includes standard definition digital formats, enhanced definition, and high definition. In this author's opinion, there are 12 HD formats (listed in Table 1.2) along with the remaining 24 ED and SD formats. Note that although there are 18 formats listed, there are actually two for each when one considers the NTSC-compatible frame rates as well as the integer frame rates. These fractional rates are designed to be compatible with the 29.97 NTSC frame rate. However, digital broadcasting does not require fractional frame rates and these will probably become obsolete as analog broadcasting comes to a close.

advanced television systems. This committee was similar to its predecessor, the National Television Standards Committee (NTSC), which established the United States' television format over 50 years ago.

The ATSC defined the 36 digital broadcast standards we have today. Twelve of these formats with the frame sizes of 720 and 1080 are high definition. Once these ATSC broadcast standards were established, manufacturers began developing and selling the production and postproduction equipment that would be compatible with them.

The ATSC broadcast table does not reflect any of the details of manu-facturers' tape formats, color space, bit depth, color sampling rates, or data compression. The ATSC table only includes the formats that are available to broadcasters for OTA broadcasting. In compari-son, NTSC is a specific process of broadcasting a composite signal. NTSC is broadcast as an analog signal with the four components of a color picture encoded into a single signal. Today's NTSC compat-ible production formats use component recording where three of the four components of the color picture are recorded separately (the fourth is derived mathematically from the other three). This component recording method is far superior to composite record-ings that were previously used. However, despite being recorded digitally, by using component processing, programs are converted to a composite signal for standard definition NTSC analog broad-casting.

This inferior method of broadcasting is now going to be replaced with the far superior digital transmission that is capable of compo-nent delivery.

On December 24, 1996, the Federal Communications Commission (FCC) formally adopted the ATSC Digital Television Standards. Despite the promise of an exciting new visual frontier, economic forces stalled the introduction of high definition video into the mainstream broadcasting and production workflow. In the past, as video technology advanced, not only did the quality improve, the cost of the new machines was also generally cheaper. High defi-nition came with a very different economic model. The large HD image along with technically complicated multi-format machines resulted in very expensive recorders/players that required new editing systems, new wiring, new sync generators, and a lot of training.

As part of the HD spectrum, there are several PAL-compatible for-mats. Even though HD has been slow to catch on with European broadcasters and consumers, more programming is becoming available both over the air and for pay TV. The three European HD formats are 720p50 720p50, 1080i25, and 1080i50. With the BBC adding more HD channels and more HD productions migrating to the PAL-compatible frame rates, the HD experience will be felt on both sides of the Atlantic.

- On a recent visit to a television repair shop, I asked the owner what he and his clients thought about the high definition revolution. His answer explained why high definition did not take off as some people had expected.
- "They started to ask some questions, but got this glazed look on their face when I tried to explain what HD was. It was too complicated. Actually, most people who buy a high definition television set do not even know how to get the HD signal into the TV. They become overwhelmed. I've discovered some people who bought a large screen HD set were watching standard definition because they didn't know how to get the HD signal into the set."
- I tell people unless they really want to see a clearer, brighter picture, they don't need high definition. It doesn't make a show any funnier or more dramatic."

As a result of all this new, complicated technology, the prices for high definition cameras, record decks, rewiring studios, redesigning machine rooms, and even the cost of a multi-format monitor were much higher than the equipment they were replacing. Broadcasters had to purchase and erect new antennas as well as create new infrastructures to handle the high definition signal.

What worsened the problem, from an economic standpoint, was the lack of interest from the consumer market. Consumers did not want to spend thousands of dollars for a new television. Without an audience, there was no reason to create HD programming. The government was pushing broadcasters to use the digital broadcast channels, but the broadcasters were merely sending standard definition programming out on the digital airwaves.

To add to the slow growth, the broadcasters had no additional income to offset the increased cost of an entirely new media path. So, in the beginning of digital broadcasting there was no incentive to pursue the production or broadcasting of high definition seriously. There was very little programming sent out on the digital frequencies, and if there was any, it was mostly standard definition NTSC.

In the past, as new videotape formats and their accompanying record decks were introduced, commercial producers were quick to use the new high tech equipment, increasing their clients' visibility, pushing the boundaries of effects, and increasing the quality of their products. Whether it was a leap from analog to digital recording formats, or the even more impressive conversion from composite recoding (a single video signal) to component recording (where three signals comprised the image), the transition was not that expensive. In addition, each new format was compatible with the existing NTSC video and broadcasting environment.

This was not the case with high definition. Advertisers, usually the first to employ new technology, saw no economic reason to support the expensive format. Only a small percentage of the population was watching digital broadcasts. The standard definition simultaneous broadcasts did not show the entire frame, and the expense for the added resolution was lost on most of the population. No one was watching and no one cared.

History had proven that consumers in the United States were not that interested in improved visual quality. After all, the United States' con-

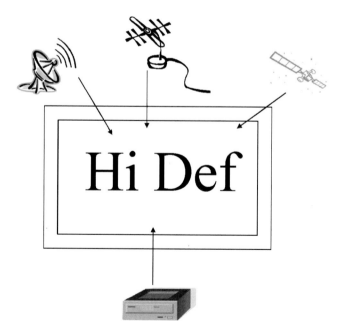

Figure 1.3 Paths to HD TV.

sumers were the ones who had chosen the cheaper, technically inferior VHS over the more expensive Betamax for their home video format.

Government Gives Additional Channels for Television Stations

Because the high definition signal required more bandwidth to broadcast its large amount of information, the United States government allocated an additional broadcast frequency to every television station in the country to accommodate their digital signal. When Congress originally assigned these digital frequencies to the television stations, the plan was to take back the old analog frequencies so they could be sold for cell phone, police, and emergency services.

Figure 1.4 Sony's XDCAM HD. This camera, introduced in 2006, records its data to an optical disk. Not only does it record the HD image, it also records a smaller copy of the footage, called a proxy, that can be used for creative editing. When the program is finished, the full size information is recaptured for the finished product, avoiding having to capture the entire amount of footage at full resolution.

However, the United States consumer was not buying the televisions capable of receiving digital broadcast signals, therefore few people were able watch what little high definition programming was available. As mentioned above, many HD sets were being sold without the capability to even receive a digital signal. These sets, called "HD ready," needed an additional piece of equipment in order to receive the digital broadcast. Manufacturers weren't making digital tuners and so the turnover, or more accurately, the shutdown, of the analog NTSC frequencies was delayed for years. No politician wanted millions of people calling to find out why their television didn't work.

By 2005, high definition had started to be of interest to the American public for several reasons. For one, the networks and pay channels began promoting their high definition productions in order to separate them from other programming choices. Consumers were being told they were missing out on something called high definition, even though they did not understand exactly what it was.

HDV Excitement

The introduction of high definition video (HDV) created a huge wave of interest with consumers, prosumers (consumers who purchase expensive, high quality consumer electronic equipment that could pass as professional) as well as professional producers and broadcasters. HDV, a very clever method of recording a high definition signal onto DV tape (the 25 Mbps tape format that popularized consumer and prosumer digital video recording), brought high definition down to a more affordable price range. In mid 2006, there were several HDV camcorders that cost under $10,000. HDV records its signal using MPEG2 compression. Also in 2006, Sony's XDCAM HD, which also uses MPEG2 encoding, was introduced. This camera, priced under $30,000 and recording its media to optical disk, put more downward pressure on the cost of shooting high definition, enticing more networks and stations to invest in HD equipment.

Now, consumers and broadcasters could shoot and edit in high definition without using a $60,000 or $90,000 camera. There were even two consumer HDV cameras for sale that were under a thousand dollars (Sony's HCR-HC1 and Sanyo's VPC-HD1).

Another factor in the acceptance of HD was that, as of July 1, 2005, Congress mandated that every television set that was 36 inches or larger, and half of all television sets 25 inches or larger, had to have digital tuners, allowing them to receive and display digital transmissions. Even through this did not require these sets to display high definition images, retailers started to promote as well as explain to consumers what digital broadcasting and high definition was all about.

With retailers and manufacturers advertising their high definition sets, networks increased the number and visibility of their high definition productions, and new televisions were now at least capable of receiving digital broadcasts.

Europe Heads Into HD Land

While the United States was forcing manufacturers to include DTV tuners in at least some of their sets, the European HD revolution was gathering its own steam. The BBC, already creating some high def programming, not only made plans to add more HD channels, it intends to produce all of its programming in HD by 2010.

One of the advantages that the European market had in starting their HD revolution after the United States was that most of the European HD broadcasters decided to use H.264/MPEG-4 AVC compression rather than the less efficient MPEG2 compression that the ATSC had defined for the United States HD digital television format. In future, the H.264/MPEG-4 AVC compression will allow Europeans to utilize their broadcast frequencies much more efficiently.

The H.264/MPEG-4 AVC compression is the format that Sony and Panasonic jointly announced as a new camcorder recording format, AVCHD, to be recorded on an 8 cm disk.

2006 seems to be the year of European HD beginning to take hold. Northern Belgium's Telenet started broadcasting HD. France's

CanalSat, M6, TPS, and TF1 all have begun HD delivery. Germany's Pro 7 and Sat 1, over-the-air broadcasters, began broadcasting HD back in 2005. As of this writing, Sky Italia intends to begin HD delivery in mid-2006. The United Kingdom company, SkyHD, also intends to begin HD broadcasting in mid-2006. The BBC has scheduled HDTV over-the-air tests in 2006.

More United States Government Mandates

The United States government, eager to retrieve the old analog television frequencies for emergency and other services, has continued to make mandates concerning the manufacturing of digital television sets. In March 2006, every television set manufactured that was 25 inches or larger was required to have digital television capability. On July 1, 2007, TVs with screens 13 inches or larger will have to be DTV-compatible. Digital broadcasting was finally being integrated into the consumers' lives, whether they liked it or not.

Digital Broadcasting is Not Necessarily HD

Another aspect of the digital video confusion comes from the fact that there are 36 digital television broadcast formats. A television equipped with a digital tuner can receive all of these formats, including the 12 that are considered high definition. In other words, with the government mandates for any set over 13 inches diagonally, a standard definition television could have the ability to receive high definition that is signal broadcast as digital television (DTV). Of course, the set could only display that image in standard definition.

Many consumers receive their video from avenues other than over the airwaves. Cable and satellite companies have joined the rush to entice individuals to support their high def line of channels. Consumers are definitely taking a much bigger interest in high definition receivers and cable/satellite offerings. The advent of HDNet, DiscoveryHD, TNTHD, HBOHD, and ShowtimeHD; NBC, CBS, and ABC producing HD shows; the volume of high definition programming and promotion; and the dropping of flatscreen prices, have enticed consumers to buy HD sets and begin watching these programs. Word of mouth is also spurring interest in HD. Neighbors who have seen the impressively clear images in high definition are telling their friends.

The United States government had intended to shut off analog broadcasting; however, there were not enough digital receivers to justify shutting off the old channels. On October 24, 2005, a United States Senate panel approved the phasing out of analog television broadcast on April 7, 2009.

This changeover to digital broadcasting does not mean all DTV will be high definition. The ATSC table allows for standard definition (SD), enhanced definition (ED), as well as high definition broadcasting. However, there is no doubt that HD production, postproduction, broadcasting, and consumer interest has blossomed.

Why Digital Broadcasting is So Important to the Government

The ATSC digital broadcasting table set the standards for United States digital broadcasting. It also allowed the transition from the NTSC frame rate of 29.97 to other integer frame rates. Once the analog broadcast frequencies are eliminated (when these frequencies are returned to the United States government), the move toward true 30 frames per second production will probably be quite rapid. The 29.97 frames per second frame rate that NTSC employs has caused a series of complications over the past 50 years. There are many professionals, including myself, who will not be sorry to see this "almost 30" format leave the production and postproduction work flow.

> People's resistance to calling frame rates exactly what they are has confused many of those people trying to understand the complexities of the high definition environment. As mentioned earlier, HD frame rates can be fractional (although these numbers are displayed with a decimal, like 29.97, 59.94, 23.98, etc.) or whole numbers (24, 30, 60).

(Continued)

> • The 18 fractional frame rates are designed to be compatible with the NTSC 29.97 frame rate. The remaining frame rates are whole numbers (24, 30, and 60 frames per second). When the NTSC analog broadcasting is terminated, there will probably be a movement toward the whole numbers as frame rates. However, the ATSC broadcast table will still list fractional frame rates, allowing these programs to be broadcast in their original format and received by digital receivers.

Here are some of the common HD terms people use when they actually mean something else:

- 24p could mean 23.98 frames per second progressive, unless the program is truly intended for a film finish. Then it *might* be a true 24 frames per second. Many film projects are still shot in 23.98, not 24.

- 50i is 50 interlaced fields, a PAL interlaced format of 25 interlaced frames, like 1080i59.94. The term "50i" indicates images per second, not frames.

- 25p represents 25 progressive frames per second, a PAL progressive format.

- 60i usually means 59.94 interlaced fields per second, yielding 29.97 interlaced frames.

- 30p usually means 29.97 progressive frames.

Broadcast Formats

The ATSC's DTV broadcast table kept fractional frame rates so that simultaneous broadcasting could exist on both the analog and digital frequencies. When all was said and done, the consortium of broadcasters and manufacturers settled on these broadcast formats, which all tuners had to be able to decode and send on to a television monitor. Most digital broadcast decoders (the ones that are sold separately from the television) can send both a high definition and a standard definition signal out of the box.

Many of the first high definition television sets were sold without the ability to receive digital signals because the devices needed to receive and decode the digital television signal (called tuners) were expensive to produce. A tuner could add over $100 to an already expensive product. As more tuners were manufactured, prices dropped for both external and internal DTV receivers.

Another reason for not including tuners in televisions was that, if a consumer intended to view high definition signals from a satellite or cable provider, a tuner was not needed. The cable or satellite company would provide the decoder, sending the high definition signal directly into the HD television using the company's equipment.

High Definition Decoder/Tuner

For over-the-air broadcast reception, a HD television needs some way to decode the digital information into a video and audio signal that the set can display. Whether this decoder/tuner is built in or is a separate unit, the device has to recognize which one of the digital signals it is receiving, then translate that signal and send it on to the device that is displaying it. Table 1.3 reveals that the decoder has a lot of processing to do. It has to figure out what signal it is receiving, and then convert it to the display monitor in either interlaced or progressive scanning

HD is a Series of Formats

An important aspect of the high definition broadcast information contained in Table 1.1 is that high definition is not a format; it is a series of formats. This family has varying sizes, frame rates, and display properties. I like to say that high def is not a format, but a family, and they don't all get along.

Why would one shoot in a high definition frame rate that could mean additional cost and potentially cause quality degradation? Footage frame rates are not always the choice of the production

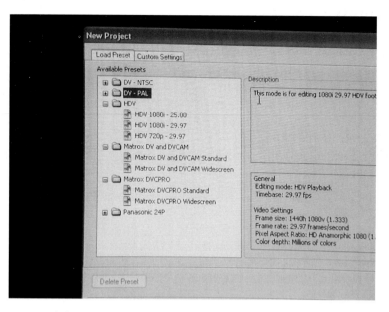

Figure 1.5 Adobe screen. The rapid acceptance of the HDV format was quickly embraced by nonlinear editors. This is a shot of a screen for opening a project in Adobe Premiere Pro version 1.5. Note that it not only is able to edit 720 and 1080 HDV formats, the version that followed (2.0) has AD-SDI and SD-SDI capabilities. Note also the frame size: 1440h x 1080v.

company. Unfortunately,sometimes footage comes from other sources and the conversion has to be made. Either the new footage is from a different source, or it could just be a misunderstanding about which frame rate was required. There are several methods for changing frame rates. Some methods are simple; others are a little more expensive and degrade the quality of the original image. These issues will be discussed in Chapter 7.

If at all possible, production footage should be shot in the delivery frame rate. If this rule is followed, and everything is shot at the same frame rate, postproduction can be much less troublesome. As mentioned earlier, one can record in 23.98, 1080psf (progressive segmented frame), and this high definition format can be converted to many other HD frame rates. Again, be forewarned: 23.98 does not have the same number of images per second as 1080i59.94, so it does not have the same look. In addition, because there are only 24 images per second (as opposed to almost 60 images per second at 1080i59.94), camera and subject movement should be carefully considered.

Formats Keep Arriving

Once video manufacturers knew the technical details of the high definition formats, they began to design machines that could record, play, and convert many of the high definition broadcast formats. In general, the "enhanced definition" formats defined by the ATSC were bypassed in favor of pursuing the complicated high definition processes. Because the ATSC digital table only defined frame rate and frame size, more recording variables came into play.

Basically, the high definition frame, whether 1080 or 720, contains a great deal of visual information. This information takes up a lot of space on videotape, computer storage disks, and/or memory chips. Manufacturers have continued in their attempts to shrink the size of the data for these large frames without sacrificing the quality of the actual image. The result was that, with the advances in technology, more and higher definition recording formats were developed.

- Drop frame time code was introduced because the color NTSC signal was not recorded or played at 30 frames a second, but just slightly less than that, at 29.97 frames per second. Counting each frame caused an error in time calculation. This caused a nightmare in editing bays as an hour of time code was an hour and 3.6 seconds in actual clock time.
- Engineers figured out a way to drop specific numbers out of the counting sequence in the NTSC time code and fixed the inaccuracy problem inherent in non-drop time code duration calculations. In the future, when analog broadcasting is stopped, digital broadcasting will have the option to use integer frame rates and leave the fractional frame rates behind. At that point, there will be no need for drop frame time code. If this becomes a reality, there would be only three frame rates: 24, 30, and 60 (and two, 25 and 50, for PAL-based broadcasters).
- When determining a final delivery frame rate, for the moment, 29.97 is probably what people mean when they talk about 30 frames per second.

Chapter One Summary

- The main purpose of this book is to explain the choices that HD offers and to point to some of the current, accepted production paths being used today.

- The high definition family offers a matrix of choices that include frame rates, frame sizes, and compression processes.

- The 1080psf23.98 format provides a great many options for format conversion.

- The particular aspects of HD are the following:

  - Frame size of either 1080 or 720 vertical lines of resolution

  - Frame rate of 23.98, 24, 29.97, 30, 59.94, or 60 frames per second

  - Bit depth of 8 bits but sometimes 10

  - Compression of various types, the most common of which is chroma subsampling

- The HD choices began when the ATSC created the digital television table of 36 digital broadcast (DTV) formats. Of those 36 formats, 12 of them are high definition.

- NBC, HDNet, Discovery HD, HBO, and CBS broadcast using 1080i59.94. ABC and ESPN air their programs in 720p 59.94.

- Progressive segmented frame recording is a progressive image that is stored as two separate fields: odd lines, then even. When the PsF image is reconstructed and displayed, it is viewed as a single progressive frame.

- Rounding frame rates to the nearest whole number can cause problems because six of the HD broadcast formats are whole numbers.

- There is no need for a tuner in an HD set if the signal is coming from a satellite provider or a cable company. In that case, the satellite or cable provider has the hardware for HD decoding.

- HDV records a high definition signal onto DV tape.

- 50i is 50 interlaced fields; a PAL interlaced format of 25 interlaced frames, like 1080i59.94, the 50i indicates images per second, not frames.

- If at all possible, production footage should be shot in the delivery frame rate.

- When determining a final delivery frame rate, 29.97 is probably what people mean when they talk about 30 frames per second.

CHAPTER 2

What Is High Definition?

The family of video formats that we call high definition was initially defined by the number of the image's horizontal lines. The common numbers used to refer to high definition size are 720 and 1080, the vertical resolution (number of horizontal lines from top to bottom) of the frame. Although a high definition frame is initially defined by its horizontal line (pixel) count, there are additional considerations within the 12 high definition formats in the ATSC table. There are even more choices when production formats that record these HD images are considered. The complicated and detailed choices that are available to shoot are what constitute the high definition production format family.

As mentioned in Chapter 1, the options in the high definition production family include the following:

- Frame size

- Frame rate

- Frame recording method

- Bit depth

- Compression

Let's examine these variables individually.

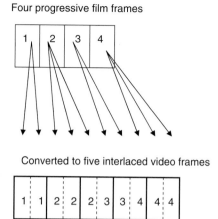

Figure 2.1 3:2 pulldown. The 3:2 pulldown process has been used for years to convert film to video. The same process is used when converting 23.98 to 29.97 video. Repeating a field of information every other frame adds the needed visual information to complete the conversion.

- As mentioned in the previous chapter, the current NTSC standard definition frame rate of 29.97 is expressed as a decimal for ease of use. The actual frame rate is calculated as 30 divided by 1.001. Thus the 29.97 is actually a fractional number, but is notated as a decimal.
- Originally, the frame rate of black and white broadcasts was a true 30 frames (or 60 fields) per second. The 29.97 frame rate was devised when engineers discovered the audio carrier signal interfered with the visual signal. By slightly reducing the frame rate, this distortion was minimized.
- In later years, it was discovered that the reduction of the frame rate created other issues. Time code, which evolved later in the history of broadcasting, counted every frame and had a built-in calculation error of 3.6 seconds per hour because there were actually less than 30 frames per second. As a result, drop frame time code was developed. Drop frame time code is time accurate.
- Another complication from the slight reduction in the frame rate of NTSC happens when transferring film to video. The frame of film (24 frames per second) being transferred to video had to be

(Continued)

slowed by 1% to 23.98 frames per second before the 3:2 pulldown was inserted to make the entire transfer compatible with NTSC's 29.97 frames per second frame rate.

One hour of calculated non-drop frame time code video is 3.6 seconds long.

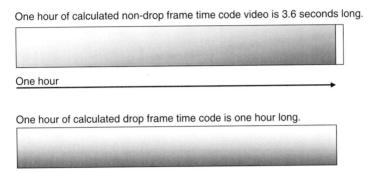

One hour of calculated drop frame time code is one hour long.

In order to create drop frame time code and make it time accurate, certain numbers were dropped. At every minute, the :00 and :01 numbers were eliminated except on the 10th minutes.

Drop frame and non drop frame time code are used in NTSC standard definition, and 1080i59.94,1080p29.97, 720p29.97.

Figure 2.2 Drop versus non-drop time code. The slight reduction in frame rate from 30 frames to 29.97 caused timing issues when time code was used to calculate durations. By dropping two numbers at every minute except the 10-minute marks (10, 20, 30, 40, 50, and 00), the error was corrected. There are no frames dropped, only numbers.

Frame Rate

Frame rate refers to the number of images stored or displayed per second. The frame rates currently being used have decimals because analog NTSC broadcasting is still in effect and most HD broadcasts are simultaneously aired in NTSC. These fractional frame rates are specifically designed to be compatible with standard definition NTSC.

For instance, a high definition 1080psf23.98 frames per second format can be converted to high definition 1080i59.94 by repeating a field of visual information every other frame (called either 3:2 or 2:3 pulldown). Some high definition decks can internally make this conversion directly out of the video deck from high definition from either 1080p23.98 to 1080i59.94 or NTSC (29.97 frames per second). Also, some nonlinear editors (NLE) can play out a 23.98 sequence at alternative frame rates.

In the near future, when analog broadcasting is terminated, it is expected that the commonly used frame rates will probably become integers as it is much easier to calculate and work with a true 24, 30, or 60 frames per second frame rate.

Currently, 720p59.94 and 1080i59.94 (a.k.a. 1080i29.97) are the commonly used high definition broadcast-destined frame rates. If a high definition production is intended to be transferred to film for projection or used in a digital intermediate process and eventually distributed on film, then either 23.98 or a true 24 frame per second progressive is used as a production frame rate.

The general consensus is that 23.98 frames per second is more film-like in its look, while the interlaced 59.94 fields per second looks more like video.

Some frame rates are not easily converted to others. Looking at the chart below, some HD machines can make direct conversions, while others have to be processed through expensive "conversion" boxes. Some machines are only capable of certain conversions if they have upgraded software, or contain optional hardware.

The best protection against unwanted or unnecessary frame conversion is to know the program's delivery format before production begins. If this is not possible, then shooting at 1080psf23.98 can provide a production frame rate that can be converted to most of the other frame rates without too much difficulty. When shooting in 23.98 frames per second, care must be taken when there is any movement, either by moving the camera or the object in the frame. With only 24 images per second, rapid movement of the camera or the subject being shot can give the appearance of strobing.

Table 2.1 HDCAM.

Original frame rate can convert to			
HDCAM 5500			
1080psf23.98	720p59.94	1080i59.94	
1080p24	1080i60		
1080psf29.97	720p59.94		
1080psf30	only itself		
1080i25	720p50		
1080i59.94	720p59.94		
1080i30	only itself		
720p50	1080i50		
720p59.94	1080i59.94		
D5			
1080psf23.98	1080i59.94	720p59.94	1080p23.98
1080psf24	1080i60	720p60	1080p24
1080p24	only itself		
1080i59.94	only itself		
720p29.97	1080i59.94		
1080i50	only itself		
1080psf25	1080p25		

This is an example of how some frame rates can be converted simply by playing a tape in a specific machine. However, not all frame rates even have conversions. These are devices that are specifically made to convert one frame rate to others.

- Feature film production has adjusted to the process of using high definition video as a production tool. Some of the movement away from film to HD as a production media is occurring because many high budget science fiction movies use computers to create the set, background, and surrounding environments in which actors perform. This means that only the actors need to be shot "in reality." The rest of the images on the screen do not exist in the real world. The actors, shot in front of a green or blue screen, are composited with computer sets, effects, and occasionally, animated characters.
- From a budget point of view, a filmmaker can shoot much more footage with video than with film. In addition, changing videotape is less frequent, less expensive, and certainly easier than changing loads of film. It should be noted, however, that shooting

(Continued)

with high definition video requires just as much attention to detail as shooting with film, perhaps even more. Costumes, pre-visualization, shot lists, background continuity, and especially lighting continue to be major considerations for the look and feel of any production, no matter what medium the images are recorded onto. In addition, if the same results are expected from high definition production as from a film production, there is no reduction in crew size or costs having to do with what happens in front of the camera lens.

Frame Recording Method

- Progressive (p)

- Interlaced (i)

- Progressive segmented (PsF)

These are the three methods of frame *recording*. However, there are only two ways to *view* them: progressive and interlaced.

A progressive frame is recorded as one continuous frame.

An interlaced recording is where the odd-numbered lines are recorded as one image, and then 1/60th of a second later, the even-numbered lines are recorded as a second image. This results in two half frames called fields. Keep in mind that only half of the frame is stored, so if the image (or the camera) moves, then two *different* images, each at half of the entire frame's resolution, are stored. The frame of two interlaced fields contains two separate, different images.

A progressive segmented recording is a combination of these two concepts. One entire frame image is captured, but is stored as two separate fields. In this way, the frame can be reconstructed and displayed as a progressive frame. Progressive segmented frame is a recording technique, not a display format.

Contrast Between Progressive and Interlaced

Consider shooting a one-second shot of a car passing, left to right, in front of the camera. Let us assume a frame rate of 29.97 frames per second at 1080 scan lines. In the progressive recording, there will be 29.97 separate, distinct images per second with 1080 lines of information in each image.

In the interlaced image, there would be 59.94 separate images with 540 lines of information in each *field*. However, a filtering process is used to eliminate flicker between the odd and even lines in the interlaced frame. As mentioned earlier, this filtering effectively reduces resolution up to 30%, thus reducing the overall 1080 image to approximately 700 lines per frame. This results in the resolution of the progressive shot having much more resolution than the interlaced one (if both of the images are the same frame size).

It becomes evident that the image quality of a particular frame rate is greatly affected by its recording method.

There is an ongoing argument concerning which has more resolution: a 1080i59.94 or a 720p59.94 image. The argument begins with the vertical image numbers. Although the 1080i59.94 frame supposedly has 1080 lines of information, in reality it only displays about 350 to 400 of the 540 lines in the video field because the resolution is significantly reduced by filtering.

There are two frame rates that are currently being used by the broadcast networks. Most of them have chosen 1080i59.94. ESPN, ABC, and Fox have opted for the 720p59.94 frame rate. The premium cable programmers (HBO, Showtime, HDNET, etc.) broadcast their shows in 1080i59.94. Their feature film presentations, however, have 3:2 pulldown introduced to bring the 23.98 film rate up to 59.94 fields per second.

Whether shooting for one of the major broadcast networks or making a film for festival submission, there are frame rates and sizes that can fit one's needs, depending on the type of look that is desired. As mentioned earlier, for a program that will eventually be scanned and then output to film, progressive 23.98 or a true 24 frames per second is the preferred choice of frame rate. (If this is one's goal, it is a good idea to contact your digital intermediate [DI] facility first and find out what they are capable of in terms of frame rate. As stated earlier, many filmmakers use 23.98 for their DI production frame rate because of its NTSC compatibility.) Many presentation projects are being shot on HDV because this format is inexpensive, looks great, and can be edited in prosumer editing systems.

- Another advantage of shooting on high definition video (versus film) is that high definition images can be played back and viewed on set immediately following the take. Most directors and producers try to arrange for a calibrated high definition monitor to be on set. This allows close examination of the take by select crew members (director, cinematographer, lighting director, continuity, etc.) to view exactly what has been shot. All questionable issues can be examined and, if necessary, the shot can be repeated. Although the ability to review shots exists on a film set, the quality of the video assist is nowhere near that of high definition.
- The informal name for the cluster of high definition equipment on set is that of a "video village." For productions with lower budgets, playback through the camera or an on-set monitor can take the place of a calibrated HD monitor. However, reviewing takes on a substandard monitor can result in missed focus issues; unwanted background action and subtle performance nuances can go unnoticed until the HD image is examined critically.

Bit Depth

Bit depth refers to the quantification of the three values that make up a high definition signal: Y, Cb, and Cr. The Y represents the luma or black and white value in the picture. Cb represents the "color difference" of blue minus luma (B-Y), and Cr is red minus luma (R-Y). With these three values, a red, green, and blue picture with luma values can be calculated and displayed.

An 8-bit depth means there are 8 bits of information for each of these three values that describe a pixel or 24 bits per pixel. An 8-bit depth allows 256 colors to be displayed at one time. A 10-bit depth allows 1024 colors to be displayed. The human eye cannot resolve much more than 1024 colors.

A 10-bit depth is "better" because a greater amount of color information is recorded, but this signal consumes much more tape/disk space. Yet for color correction latitude and effects (green screen, blue screen, color correction), 10 bit is preferable for high-end HD productions. Most broadcasters consider 8 bit adequate for production, whereas filmmakers want 10 or even 12 if possible.

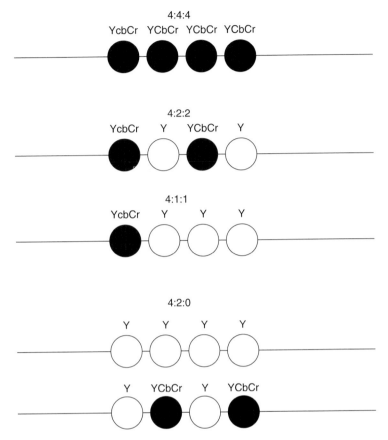

Figure 2.3 Color subsampling. The elimnation of color information is commonly used to lower the amount of information to be recorded. HDV with its severe subsampling gets the data rate low enough to transmit via firewire, and it can be recorded on standard DV tape.

Even though the human eye cannot see much past 10-bit video color, computer programs make use of the extra color information. Color is especially critical when creating green and blue screen effects. It is more difficult to properly key these types of effects when HDV is used because much of the color information is literally thrown away as HDV is recorded to videotape.

High definition video is usually shot at 8 or 10 bit, with 8 being the more common and considered acceptable for broadcast color display choice. Most feature film productions record 10-bit depth.

This is because the DI process requires that minimum level of color depth for color correction and effects.

- Again, the immediacy of HD has its advantage. It is not uncommon for an editor to be located either on set or near the production location. As soon as a reel of footage is shot, it can be dubbed to a workprint format, delivered to the editor, and cut into the scene. Rather than waiting for the lab to deliver film dailies and then discovering that critical footage is needed or that new shots are required, an on-set editor can make this determination within hours of the completion of a shot or scene, often while the crew is still at that particular location.
- The net result is that one can shoot at 23.98 or 24 frames per second; light a scene as well as in a film production; edit on an electronic system, quite possibly on the set; and confirm the acceptability of the shot immediately. With the postproduction workflow of high definition-to-film established and becoming less and less expensive, filmmakers are looking at high definition as an acceptable if not, in many cases, superior alternative to film acquisition.

Chroma Subsampling

Before color television was officially adopted, a great deal of experimentation took place to find out exactly how much color a human actually sees. It was discovered that humans are far more sensitive to the black and white portion of an image than to the color aspects. As video recording schemes progressed, color information was usually the first part of an image that was compromised, much more so than the luminance information because humans could not tell that portion of the image was missing. The process of recording less chroma than the luma portion of the image is a form of compression called chroma subsampling.

By eliminating a portion of the color information in an image, the amount of data that has to be stored is reduced. Chroma sampling in the digital video world is designated by three numbers in the following format:

X:X:X (Luma:Cr:Cr)

For instance, 4:4:4 indicates that the luma portion of the signal is sampled at the same rate as the two chroma components. (HD video is in a YCbCr color scheme.) The first 4 indicates the y or luma portion of the signal, the next two numbers describe the CbCr sampling ratio to the luma.

A 4:2:2 indicates the luma is sampled four times, while the chroma is being sampled at half that rate. Essentially, this type of color sampling throws half of the color information away. A 4:2:0 (MPEG2 HD, MPEG4 HD) is somewhat misleading as both the Cb and Cr are sampled but only every other line. In other words, the luminance is sampled every line, but the chroma is not sampled on the first line (4:0:0), but is sampled on the next one (4:2:2). A 4:0:0 color sampling scheme is used for standard definition DV recording.

As less information is recorded, the amount of information decreases and less disk space or tape is needed to store the image. Feature film high definition production will usually record 4:4:4 because the image will be projected and all the color information that can be stored is considered necessary, due to the high demand for color information in special effects and color correction.

There is also a fourth number that can be included in the color sampling scheme, written in the following format:

X:X:X:X (Luma:Cr:Cr:Alpha)

- Color is treated differently in different applications. In video, luma and two color difference components, are based on blue minus luma and red minus luma. However, the red, blue, and luma are subject to different gamma correction depending on how the information is to be displayed. HD is in the YcbCr scale (although many incorrectly think it is YUV). YUV is not appropriate to component video; it is used in single signal transmissions like NTSC or PAL. However, the mislabeling of YUV has become so common and misused that YUV has come to erroneously mean "any video represented by Y, R-Y and B-Y".

This last number would indicate an alpha channel, which is a black and white signal designed to "hold out" visual information from a background. This number is usually a 4 because alpha channels should be of high quality.

4:2:2 is a widely used color subsampling in NTSC. Digital BetaCam records its NTSC images in a 4:2:2 color space.

Compression

Compression is an overall description of many possible processes that convert video into a digital code that takes up less transmission space than the original signal would have otherwise used. Color subsampling of luminance and chrominance is one form of compression. Some nonlinear editors have the option of compressing the video signal (again) on input. Some high-end editing systems edit 1:1, which means that there is no compression on input, yet the signal is almost always compressed during the recording (production) process through color subsampling and data compression. As we have stated before, an uncompressed, full frame HD signal is very large; a full frame of 1080i59.94 HD takes 1.3 gigabytes of storage. It is economically unfeasible to use this amount of data as a production or postproduction medium.

The compromise is to compress this information into a form that does not degrade the image too much. As technology has progressed, many different methods of compression have evolved so that a frame of HD can be stored, depending on the image requirements.

There are degrees of compression. At the high-end of compression you would have an HDV image. On the other end is a full 4:4:4 data (not video) recording, like those used in extremely high-end feature film production using HD cameras that feed dual drive computer recorders.

In the HD middle ground, the D5 recording format uses a 4:1 compression at 8-bit color and 5:1 at 10 bit. The HDCAM records 8-bit,

3:1:1 subsampling with 1440 horizontal lines, resulting in a 7.1:1 compression ratio. HDCAM SR (superior recording) uses a 10-bit recording format with 4:2:2 recording the compression ratio of 2.7/1; in 4:4:4 recording the compression ratio is 4.2:1. DVCPRO-HD is 8-bit 4:2:2 subsampled and results in a 6.7:1 compression.

As noted earlier, much of this compression, especially that of the color subsampling, is not apparent to the human eye, and engineers continue to work on shrinking the size of high definition images, while preserving the image's quality.

Putting It Together

With so many choices, one wonders how to choose a high definition format for a particular project. There can be several correct answers to this question, but there is one phrase that should be remembered: the delivery format determines the production format.

The Production Choice

Although it is probably dangerous and somewhat presumptuous to predict what formats to use, especially considering that a week before delivering this manuscript a new recording format was announced as well as three new HDV cameras just two weeks after, I will risk being wrong and list what I would use for a particular project.

If you do not know the delivery format, and you cannot find out what it is, I would shoot at 1080psf23.98. Using this format, the program could be converted to almost any of the other formats including our video standard for over 50 years, NTSC. Be fore-warned, however, that some networks are very particular not only about their delivery formats, but also what production formats are used in the postproduction treatment of that original camera for-mat. In addition, make sure you review any shot with movement, even walking or panning, as the 23.98 frame rate has only 40% of the individual images as 720p59.94 or 1080i59.94. This difference in frames per second is very apparent in movement of any kind.

It is always a good idea to double-check production, editing, and delivery technicalities when working in high definition and especially when using HDV as a production source. All purchasers of high definition programming have clearly stated guidelines concerning both production and post production requirements. At the very least, communication with the client about how the production is going to be shot and how it is going to be edited (including nonlinear editor input codecs) must be discussed before too much (expensive) editing and potential conversion consumes the production's budget.

The choice of production frame rate and frame size is usually the same as the delivery format. Bit rate would be either 8 or 10, depending on production footage or delivery specifications. Once a tape is shot at an 8-bit rate, there is no way to turn that image into a true 10-bit image. The color information has not been recorded and cannot be recreated. It will always stay at 8 bit. Color sampling is created when the image is recorded. Once the chroma information is lost, it cannot be recovered. At this point in time, 4:2:2 is consid-

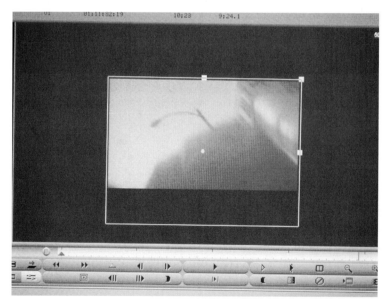

Figure 2.4 Adjusting 4 × 3 in 16 × 9 space. When placing a 4 × 3 standard definition image in a 16 × 9 HD frame, the bottom of the frame is the part usually eliminated.

ered a standard in broadcast high definition production. HDCAM, which records 3:1:1 and 1440 lines, is also a popular production format.

All things being equal (which they never are), one would shoot and edit with the highest quality available (always taking into consideration the delivery format).

If the footage is being supplied by another production company, there may not always be a postproduction choice. If the footage is already shot, the existing footage may determine the editing parameters. For instance, if the entire piece was shot in standard definition NTSC and the delivery format is intended to be in high definition, the program should probably be edited in standard definition NTSC and then the entire program should be blown up (enlarged) after editing.

Another example of postproduction planning would be if the delivery format was 1080i59.94 and half the program was shot in 1080psf23.98 and half in 1080i59.94. Down-converting the 59.94i footage would visibly hurt the program, so it seems logical to edit the program in 1080i59.94. The portion of the program that was shot in the 23.98 frame rate would be best served by importing from the video deck as 1080i59.94. The 1080psf23.98 footage is created by adding fields (2:3 pulldown) on playback and the nonlinear editing would capture the footage as 1080i59.94.

Mixing SD and HD

What if there is a mixture of high definition and standard definition NTSC formats but delivery is to be in high definition? The ideal situation would be to edit in the highest level of production footage to preserve the image quality and to simplify frame rate conversions. If delivery was 1080i59.94 but some of the footage was shot at 720p23.98 high definition, 1080i59.94, and NTSC, the best way to edit this program would be to edit in 1080i59.94. This option allows for introducing 3:2 pulldown to the 720p footage and resizing the NTSC footage.

It must be noted here that standard definition (SD) is a 4 × 3 ratio and HD is 16 × 9. To integrate SD into a high def project, there has to be some adjustment. Usually the SD is increased to fill the horizontal frame lines and then moved vertically to reveal the best portion of the 4 × 3 image, most often eliminating the bottom of the SD frame.

The one situation not discussed so far is when a delivery is 1080psf23.98 and there are higher frame rates (1080i59.94 or 720p29.97) involved. This presents a complicated postproduction challenge. If the interlaced 1080i59.94 footage or progressive 720p29.97 footage is not of great length, it can be converted to the lower frame rate through a frame conversion device. The conversion is expensive and slightly blurs the image, but is coming down in price.

If there is a large amount of footage, it might be prudent to call the purchasing company and see if a higher delivery frame rate would be acceptable.

Figure 2.5 SD versus HD sizing. A standard definition frame is much smaller than an HD frame. Here is an example of how small the SD image really is.

High Definition Production Choice Summary

High definition production choices are usually defined by the delivery specifications. The choices for HD include the following:

Size, which is designated by horizontal lines:
  Either 1080 or 720
Frame rates:
  23.97, 24, 29.97, 30, 59.94, or 60
Frame recording method:
  Interlaced, progressive, or segmented progressive
Color bit depth:
  8 or 10 bits
Color sampling (usually subsampling):
  Examples include 4:4:4, 4:2:2, 4:1:1, 3:1:1, 4:0:0, and 4:2:2:4

Choosing the production format is another challenge. The current mainstream HD recording formats are HDCAM, HDCAM SR, DVCPRO-HD, and D5.

Everything is Changing

This is the beginning of a video revolution. High definition is being accepted by consumers, manufacturers, and broadcasters. But like the early days of any new technology, experiments are made, shortcuts are taken, discoveries are revealed, and only in hindsight will we know what really worked and what was thrown away.

Ultimately, consumers make the choice. Betamax was eliminated as a home format as consumers chose technically inferior yet cheaper VHS. Who knows what will happen with high definition?

Some new experiments and shortcuts become established postproduction paths; some do not. In the past year, entire lines of HD cameras have been introduced. Almost all nonlinear editing systems have introduced upgraded HD and HDV editing capability, and more offerings are on the way. With consumers and retailers interested in HD, production has increased, and there are updates and new equipment being introduced every month.

When HD is Not True HD: Uprezing Video to HD

Like any other video format, images from other sources can be recorded onto a high definition tape. However, this does not make the recorded image HD. As high definition programming becomes much more commonplace, the mixing of HD and NTSC images will occur more often, especially with programming that includes historical footage.

If one is going to mix high definition with NTSC images, it is best to get the highest quality NTSC images available. NTSC has many of its own variations: VHS, three-quarter inch, one inch, BetaCam, Beta Sp, MII, D2, Digital BetaCam, and so forth. Since the NTSC image will be viewed alongside the HD content, obtaining the highest quality NTSC image is advisable.

Since NTSC is shot and edited in a 4 × 3 format, some producers choose to keep their NTSC images in the 4 × 3 ratio, especially if these images are of historical value, rather than cutting off the top and bottom of the frame in order to fit it into the 16 × 9 high definition display format. Another solution is to place the NTSC image on top of a high definition, full frame graphic. This allows the entire high definition frame to be filled with video, avoiding view confusion, yet still maintaining the NTSC 4 × 3 ratio.

Table 2.2 shows the huge amount of storage needed for uncompressed video. Certain editing systems can compress video during capture, reducing the space required for storage. Before using these codecs, one should check with the company buying the production to make sure that the compression scheme is acceptable.

Table 2.2 Examples of one hour uncompressed 4:2:2 video storage needs.

Frame size	Frame rate	Bit depth	Storage
1080	23.98	8	342 GB (358)
1080	23.98	10	427 GB (478)
1080	29.97	8	427 GB (448)
1080	29.97	10	534 GB (597)
720	23.98	8	152 GB (159)
720	23.98	10	190 GB (215)
720	29.97	8	190 GB (199)
720	29.97	10	237 GB (269)

Figure 2.6 The storage requirement for HD is much larger than that of SD. This is a photo of two rows of local RAID array on top of the hardware for a Symphony Nitris HD editing system.

Budget Considerations

If cost was not an issue, producers would rent the best camera, record on the best video deck at the highest resolution, and edit their programs in the highest image quality with the best edit system available using unlimited computer storage. The real production world deals with real-world costs every day, and the delivery workflow process determines many of the high definition choices that producers make: is it cost effective? Will the show be visually acceptable? Is there enough hard drive space to complete the project, and how much will it cost just to store that media an extra three weeks when changes come in?

It is important to note, even though high definition is often a videotape-based format, there are other considerations that affect image quality. Lighting, lenses, cameras, as well as the technical aspects of the high definition camera operation can hurt or enhance the visual image being recorded.

Computer File Size for High Definition Video

There is no doubt that high definition digital media, even when compressed, takes up a lot of computer hard drive space. Consider a feature film with 50 hours of production material. To store all this material at a 10:1 compression ratio would still take almost 2,000 gigabytes (2 terabytes) of media storage. This calculation only considers the media needed for the creative editing process. Additional storage would still be needed for graphics media, titles, pickup shots, and effects renders. Render files are created as the non-linear computer editor manufactures (renders) non-real-time effects.

When it comes to finishing this hypothetical production in high definition, a 90-minute show at full 1080i59.94, 10-bit resolution with little or no effect work would require about 900 gigabytes of storage. And again, this calculation of disk space does not take into account multilayered effects, titles, and full resolution graphics.

To add to the storage requirements for a project, it is a basic editing rule never to fill a computer drive past 90% of capacity. If a hard drive is filled past 90%, it has a difficult time locating and accessing necessary information in the time required. Dropped frames, slow response, and poor editing capabilities are the results of a full hard drive.

A show that requires 900-gigabytes of media storage would need at least a terabyte of hard disk storage to access the show's images effectively and probably another 200 "gigs" of additional storage for the program's other image needs (graphics, titles and effect renders).

Conversion Problems

Consider shooting a one-second shot of a car passing by the camera with a frame rate of 29.97 frames per second. Now think about having to deliver that one-second shot at 23.98 frames per second. Six frames have to be eliminated from the shot. Which ones are to be eliminated? And think about the shot itself—the fluid aspect of the car moving across the frame is definitely going to be altered.

In this digital age, with very clever programs and highly compli-cated video decks, the frame conversion process has improved dra-matically. There are devices that convert one frame rate to another. The results are impressive, but they come with an additional cost, and some degradation of the original image's quality.

True Versus Converted Frames

Let us take another example of the one-second car shot passing in front of the camera. We will shoot at 1080i59.94. Now we are told we will have to deliver the shot at 720p (progressive) at 59.94 frames per second. The good news is that we have the same frame rates, and the newer, smaller frame size is an easy conversion. If we transfer this footage to a HDCAM, the tape machine can do the conversion internally and output a 720p59.94 master. But how does the conversion occur from an interlaced image to a progres-sive one? If one shoots a true progressive frame, only a single image is recorded. In this case, the converted single progressive frame is actually a combination of the two interlaced fields. The result is not readily apparent as the program plays, but stopping at an individual frame will show the "melded" combination. Again, with static shots or those with little movement, there is no discernible difference because the interlaced frame contains basically the same information. When there is movement, the interlaced frame is readily apparent by stopping and freezing an individual frame.

A word of warning: the delivery of an interlaced program masquer-ading as a progressive show may cause the entire program to be rejected.

How to Choose an HD Format for a Particular Show

Once producers, directors, and production companies realized that high definition was a family of formats, and there were no real guidelines for the choices that were offered, the issue then became, which format was the best?

Figure 2.7 HD productions have made high quality presentation productions very affordable. This is a still from *That Guy,* an HD production that was shot in Hollywood. (Photo courtesy of Eyekandy Productions. Photo by Breht Gardner.)

It basically comes down to the fact that there is no "best" format. Some individuals like the 23.98 with its film look. Others like the 1080i59.94 with its video look. And many budget-conscious filmmakers like HDV with its low tape cost and ability to edit in prosumer nonlinear editors.

Nevertheless, in the final analysis, the delivery format determines the production format.

Offline/Online Edit System Compatibility

In the early days of nonlinear editing it was very difficult to use one program for creative editing, then another for conforming that project. To this day, most professionals will not cross platform (go from one editing computer program to another). Despite many similar plugins and software conversion programs, they know that unless the program is a series of simple cuts, like a dramatic film, the conform should be performed on the same software that was used to creatively cut it.

In high def, similar problems and complications arise. Transferring between editing programs can cause a great deal of effects issues. Unless your program is composed of cuts, it is best not to cross platforms from creative editing systems to the conforming program if it is at all possible.

If you do have to creatively edit on one format and conform on another, there are software programs to "translate" from one edit system to another. Automatic Duck is one of the better known of these programs.

Nonlinear Editors With No Frame Rate Restrictions

There are programs that will accept any frame rate into their time line. Yet if a frame rate is dropped into a project that is different from that of the original project, how is that conversion going to take place? Some programs adjust the frame rate automatically; others require one or more effects to adjust the way the footage plays. It is not always a drag-and-drop solution. Just because a clip can be placed on a time line, it does not mean it is playing at the proper speed or will stay in sync with the audio.

HD is Looking Good

The high definition format family offers a series of choices that can satisfy the filmmaker, the broadcaster, and the experimenter. Which one is more appealing is often a judgment call that professionals and viewers do not always agree on. There are those who love the look of 23.98, which is more film-like. Others like 59.94i, which looks more like video and may seem more familiar to a television viewer. Still others choose a middle ground of 29.97p.

Lossy Versus Lossless Compression

Compression is a method of taking a digital file and making it smaller. Then later, when that file is decompressed, the issue becomes whether all the original data still exist.

Lossy compression is a method of compressing a file, but when that file is restored it has less information than when it started.

Lossless compression is one that restores to 100% of its original form.

It is interesting to note that shooting in DVCPRO HD or HDV, or XDCAM HD, or importing HD through the use of a codec (like DNxHD) can lower the storage requirement a great deal. Also, with a frame rate of 23.98 and/or a frame size of 720, the storage requirement is significantly lower than at 1080i59.94.

- There is no doubt that high definition with its many production choices has caused a great deal of confusion. Considering all the issues HD has created, I would like to offer a high definition acronym: CCEC (Constant Communication and Equipment Check).
- One of the major pitfalls in high definition productions is that not only is HD confusing, there also seems to be a lack of communication among everyone involved. To make matters worse, HD equipment is inherently complicated and has many, many settings. I cannot tell you how many times I have been saved by asking the same question several times, over and over, about whether particular compression codecs are permissible, or whether this graphic is the most current one, or whether this reel is really a high definition source. The questions may seem to be endless and all too often silly, and the answers are often very necessary to the person finishing the project and obvious to the person who edited the piece.
- A producer who communicates with the postproduction supervisor or editor before shooting in HD will probably be much happier in the long run. Many feature film producers have editors and postproduction coordinators on the set, or at least within reach so that the production issues will not make a mistake with their frame rates or camera settings. After all, without postproduction, production would never see the light of a TV or projector lamp.

Figure 2.8 HDCAM SR. The HDCAM SR has become one of the standard studio HD recorders.

Shoot, Edit, and Deliver at One Frame Rate—What a Concept

Producing all material of a specific program at the same frame rate, and at the same frame size and bit depth, is a godsend. To stay organized and shoot every location at the same frame rate is one of the best ways to avoid postproduction problems (CCEC).

Some nonlinear editors will not allow mixing of certain frame rates, and many will not mix progressive and interlaced formats. It often happens that different materials are used in a show, but if it is possible, one frame rate is the way to go in HD.

Chapter Two Summary

- The common numbers used to refer to high definition formats are 720 and 1080. These refer to the vertical resolution of the frame.

Figure 2.9 Adobe Bay. Affordability in nonlinear edit systems has sped up the acceptance of HD and HDV productions. This is a photo of an Adobe Premiere Pro editing system. (Photo courtesy of New Wave Entertainment.)

- The ATSC digital broadcast table defines 36 frame sizes and frame rates as the United States' digital television formats (DTV).

- Twelve of these digital broadcast formats fall into the category of high definition. The ATSC DTV table provides for two sizes of high definition images: 720 (vertical) by 1280 (horizontal) lines and 1080 (vertical) by 1920 (horizontal) lines of resolution.

- The options in the high definition production family include the following:

  - Frame rate

  - Frame recording method

- Bit depth

- Compression

- Drop frame time code is time accurate.

- Non-drop time code is not time accurate

- Currently, 720p59.94 and 1080i59.94 (a.k.a. 1080i29.97) are the commonly used high definition broadcast-destined frame rates.

- The general consensus is that 23.98 frames per second is more film-like in its look, while the interlaced 59.94 fields per second looks more like video.

- The best protection is to know the delivery format before production begins.

- Shooting at 1080psf23.98 can provide a production frame rate that can be converted to most of the others without too much difficulty.

- When shooting in 23.98 frames per second, care must be taken when there is any movement, either from moving the camera itself, or shooting objects that move in the frame.

- Frame recording methods include the following:

  - Progressive (p)

  - Interlaced (i)

  - Progressive segmented (psf)

- The above are the three methods of frame *recording*. Although there are three frame recordings, there are only two ways to *view* them: progressive or interlaced.

- A progressive frame is recorded as one continuous frame.

- An interlaced recording is where the odd-numbered lines are recorded, and then 1/60th of a second later, the even-numbered lines are recorded. This results in two half frames called fields.

- An interlaced recording has two *different* images per frame.

- A progressive segmented recording is a combination of these two concepts. The entire frame image is captured, but is stored as two separate fields. In this way, the frame can be reconstructed and displayed as a progressive frame.

- Progressive segmented frame is a recording technique, not a display format.

- Bit depth refers to the quantization of the three values that make up a high definition signal: Y, Cb, and Cr.

  - Y represents the luma or black and white value in the picture.

  - Cb represents the "color difference" blue minus luma (B-Y).

  - Cr is red minus luma (R-Y).

- An 8-bit depth means there are 8 bits of information for each of these three values that describe a pixel. An 8-bit depth allows 256 colors to be displayed at one time. A 10-bit depth allows 1024 colors to be displayed.

- Many broadcast producers feel that high definition production with a bit depth of 8 is more than adequate for network delivery.

- 4:4:4 indicates that the luma portion of the signal is sampled at the same rate as the two chroma components.

- 4:2:2 indicates the luma is sampled four times, while the chroma is being sampled at half that rate.

- 4:2:0 indicates the luminance is sampled every line, while the chroma is not sampled on the first line (4:0:0) but is sampled on the next one (4:2:2).

- A fourth number can be included in the color sampling scheme and is written in the following format:

$$X:X:X:X$$

This last number would indicate an alpha channel, which is a black and white signal designed to "hold out" visual information from a background.

4:2:2 is a widely used color subsampling in NTSC.

Color subsampling of luminance and chrominance is one form of compression.

Some networks are very particular not only about delivery formats, but also production formats as well as the postproduction treatment of the original camera format.

To integrate SD into a high def project, there has to be some adjustment. The SD is increased to fill the horizontal frame lines and then moved vertically to reveal the best portion of the 4 × 3 image, most often eliminating the bottom of the SD frame.

High Definition Production Choice Summary

- Production choices include size, which is designated by horizontal lines:

  - Either 1080 or 720

- Frame rates:

  - 23.97, 24, 29.97, 30, 59.94, or 60

- Frame recording method:

- Interlaced, progressive, or segmented progressive

- Color bit depth:

  - 8 or 10 bits

- Color sampling (usually subsampling):

  - Examples include 4:4:4, 4:2:2, 4:1:1, 3:1:1, 4:0:0, and 4:2:2:4

- The current mainstream HD recording formats are the following: HDCAM, HDCAM SR, DVCPRO-HD, and D5.

- One should never fill a computer drive past 90% of capacity.

- The delivery format determines the production format.

- Unless your program is composed of cuts, do not cross platforms if it is at all possible.

- Shoot, edit, and deliver at one frame rate, the delivery rate if possible.

CHAPTER 3
Myths and Questons About HD

With its numerous frame rates, frame sizes, and different production formats, high definition can be very confusing. This chapter contains a series of commonly asked questions followed by answers that should help clarify some of the concepts and uses of high definition.

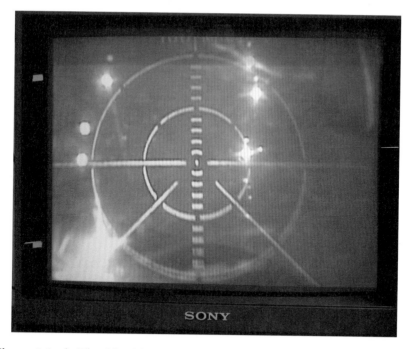

Figure 3.1a, b The 16 × 9 HD image in a Standard Definition space can be placed in several different ways. (a) It can be centered with the top and bottom edges reaching the top and bottom of the 4 × 3 (sometimes called a center extraction).

(Continued)

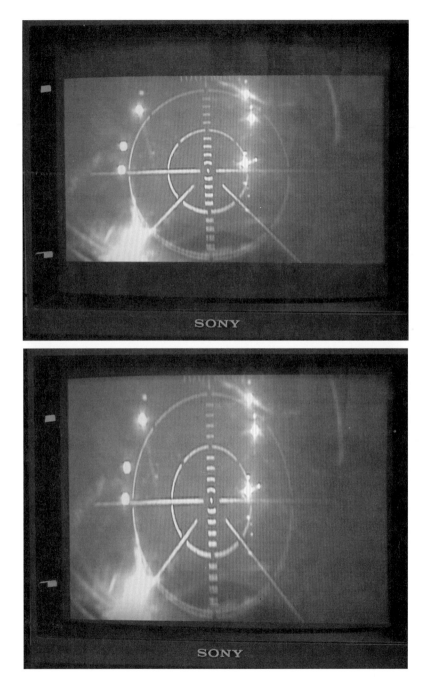

Figure 3.1 Cont'd (b) It can be placed side to side in the 4 × 3 space with black margins at the top and bottom (sometimes called letterboxed) (c) Or it can be vertically stretched, usually for DVD delivery, which then returns it to 16 × 9 on playback. (Called either 16 × 9 stretched, enhanced, or 16 × 9 anamorphic.)

Can HD Be Seen on a Regular Television?

Technically, yes. Images shot in high definition can be viewed on a regular or "standard definition" television, but the high definition image has to be altered in order to be compatible with the NTSC size and frame rate (NTSC is 720 × 486 lines displayed at 29.97 interlaced frames per second).

Because the original high definition signal is recorded in a 16 × 9 format and standard definition NTSC's display format is in a 4 × 3 ratio, some kind of change must be made. There are several options to view the 16 × 9 high definition image on a 4 × 3 television set.

One method of viewing high definition on a 4 × 3 set is to shrink the HD image so that the entire 16 × 9 frame is viewed. This reduction of the 16 × 9 image leaves black bars, or margins, at the top and bottom of the 4 × 3 screen image. This type of image is called "letterboxed."

Another way to view a high definition image on a standard definition television or monitor is to eliminate a portion of the 16 × 9 frame at the sides. In this way, the entire 4 × 3 screen is filled. Sometimes, rather than just eliminating the sides of the 16 × 9 frame, effects can be used to pan the image left or right, centering on the most important part of the action in the 4 × 3 frame. Nonlinear editors and digital video effects devices can be used to pan the 16 × 9 image before it is recorded in standard definition. Once the image is recorded on the 4 × 3 tape, there is extra image space on the sides of the frame .

The act of selectively moving the widescreen image left and right for full-screen viewing in 4 × 3 is called "pan and scan."

This method has been used for years when transferring widescreen movies to 4 × 3 NTSC format tape. In the case of transferring film to tape, a telecine (film to tape) machine scans the film, and the operator pans the image left or right to show the most important or relevant portion of the scene. One reason the pan and scan process was used was because viewers thought they were missing part of the picture when a letterboxed image was broadcast. They thought that the black bars at the top and bottom of the screen were caused by a flaw in the transmission or signal.

A third method of transferring 16 × 9 high definition is to stretch the image vertically while keeping the 16 × 9 image from reaching the edges of the frame. This process fills the entire 4 × 3 screen with the 16 × 9 image from top to bottom. Called 16 × 9 anamorphic, 16 × 9 stretched or 16 × 9 enhanced, the idea is that by stretching the image, the entire 4 × 3 screen is used for the image, and when it is compressed for viewing, the resolution is improved (compared to a 4 × 3 letterboxed image).

As audiences have become accustomed to the black mask at the top and bottom of the screen, fewer movies and other programs shot

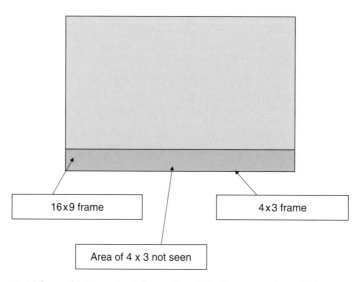

Figure 3.2 When placing a 4 x 3 frame in a 16 x 9 space, often the bottom of the frame is eliminated, moving the 4 x 3 image downward.

in widescreen formats are being panned and scanned. Instead, the image is reduced to show the entire widescreen image. There are still many times where a widescreen movie is broadcast full frame, but most often the beginning and end of the movie are letterboxed because there is no way to pan and scan a title or credits that reach across the screen.

No matter what, when a high definition image is displayed on an NTSC 4 × 3 screen, that image will be of substantially lower quality than the original high def image.

Why Are There So Many High Definition Frame Rates?

When the ATSC was formulating its broadcast table, many viewpoints were considered, and all kinds of video users were consulted. Manufacturers and professionals demanded different types HD formats for different "looks" and different economic purposes. Rather than ignore the requests of these different groups, the ATSC DTV table was designed to satisfy many different needs of video and film users.

As a result of these varying demands, six distinct flavors of high definition were created. The reason there are 12 HD formats is that six are compatible with the NTSC frame rate. The remaining six ignore the 1% slowdown to accommodate NTSC and are frame rates of whole numbers.

Considering the six basic frame rates, many film style advocates wanted 24 (23.98) and 30 (29.97) frames per second frame rates with progressive scanning. Others wanted to preserve the interlaced frames at 30 frames (59.94) to mimic the current NTSC look. Some broadcasters wanted 60 (59.94) frames per second progressive because they felt this was a better way to view sporting events. In other words, the ATSC DTV table attempted to satisfy a group of demands, not a single one.

Of course, after 50 years of creating and storing hundreds of thousands of hours of original NTSC material, the ability to broadcast the NTSC frame rates not only ensured a smooth transition to DTV, the NTSC programs can also continue to be aired on the digital broadcast channels.

Why Did Congress Delay Turning Off the NTSC Broadcast Channels?

The United States consumers were extremely slow in replacing their working NTSC televisions with more expensive and often misunderstood digital television sets. There was also the problem that many of the early high definition sets were sold without the ability to receive HD. These sets, called "HD ready" could display an HD signal, but could not decode digital broadcasts.

As a result of the consumers refusing to switch their televisions, the government delayed the handover of the analog television broadcast frequencies. Officials were concerned that if they "turned off" regular television without enough people able to receive digital broadcasts, many consumers would be angry.

- One producer had a very important high definition project that was to be projected on a large screen to prospective clients at a conference. Three of the four segments of the program were created by the producer at 1080p23.98.
- The fourth segment was created and delivered by a separate company that did not communicate with the producer. Days before the conference, the fourth and final section arrived. It had been shot and edited in high definition, but at 1080i59.94 (1080i29.97). At great expense, the fourth segment was converted to 1080p23.98, the frame rate of the other three segments. The presentation was shown through the use of a video projector across a very large auditorium. It was apparent that the converted portion of the program was far from perfect and was much less clear than the rest of the show.
- As I have said previously, "HD is not a format but a family, and they don't all get along."

Is Digital TV HD?

The image you see displayed on a digital television may not be high definition. Standard definition signals (SD) and enhanced definition signals (ED) are also part of the ATSC digital broadcast format that stations are allowed to transmit. Another possibility is that the HD television could be receiving standard definition programming from a cable or satellite provider. In order to display an HD signal, the high definition signal has to arrive at the consumer's home, be decoded, and then be set on to the television.

In most cases, high definition televisions have several options for video inputs. However, many people who have purchased digital televisions do not realize that they need to switch the input to display HD. This is why so many people who have bought HD TVs end up watching really big standard definition programming.

Is Uncompressed the Best Way to Shoot HD?

Maybe so, but to record an uncompressed HD signal is incredibly expensive. A single frame of uncompressed 1080i29.97 is about 1.5 gigabytes worth of information, far beyond the needs (and budget) of most broadcast productions. It actually comes down to the definition of "best." For many, many productions, D5, HDCAM,

Figure 3.3 HD decoder. This is a Samsung HD over-the-air decoder. It has a standard definition output, and two frame size outputs, 720 and 1080. This is only used for DTV reception. For cable or satellite HD conversions, there are different conversion boxes.

XDCAM, DVCPRO HD, HDCAM SR, and even HDV can be acceptable for production purposes.

These production formats and recorders use some sort of compression combined with color subsampling (recording less color
information than luminance) as a way to keep the video files man-
ageable, and they have been proven acceptable for HD productions.
Asking for uncompressed HD video for broadcast is like asking for
a Formula One race car to drive on a freeway. You can do it, but it is
not really necessary.

Is HD Digital TV?

Sometimes a high definition signal is DTV, and sometimes it
isn't. Digital TV is a digital format that is broadcast from an
antenna, over the airwaves, and then received at the consumer's
tuner. The tuner then converts the DTV signal and feeds it to
the television screen. In many cases, a DTV signal from a station

Figure 3.4 The Sony high def Handycam™ Camcorder, another example
of how the HD revolution has invaded even the consumer market. Just
as DV revolutionized the home video market, HDV is already making a
huge impact.

contains no high definition but one or more standard definition signals.

Do Television Stations Always Broadcast the Same Signal on Their Digital and Analog Channels?

Not always. Some stations broadcast the same program simultaneously on their analog and digital frequencies. However, many stations broadcast up to five separate standard definition signals on the same digital channel. The ability to use a particular digital frequency for additional SD signals allows the station to sell more commercial time on its frequency. A broadcast station has many options as to what type and how many signals it can broadcast on its digital channel. A broadcaster could be airing five standard definition programs for one hour, then switch to a single high def program in the next, and then do one HD program, yet all the time, they could be airing a completely different program on their analog channel. Until the government takes back the analog frequencies from the Unites States television stations, they have the choice of what to air on either of their assigned frequencies.

Is HDV the Same Quality as HD?

Before answering this question, let's review what HD is.

For the purpose of this discussion, HD is one of the 12 broadcast-compatible formats described in the ATSC table. HDV falls into that description.

As discussed earlier, an uncompressed frame of HD is far too large to be commercially considered for production. So, that frame of information is manipulated in many different ways to be visually acceptable and yet not take up too much bandwidth.

HDV happens to be one of the most compressed versions of HD. It is still of high quality and is considered to be HD. HDV is recorded on a standard DV tape at a bit rate of 19Mbs for the 720 by 1280 progressive signal, or 25Mbs for the 1080 × 1440 interlaced frame. The 1080 frame rate is played out at 1080 × 1920. This scheme of recording the 1080 × 1440 and playing out at 1080 × 1920 is also used by Sony's HDCAM, but not the HDCAM SR.

Is High Definition Recorded the Same Way on All HD Machines?

No, not at all. Each manufacturer has developed its own particular methods of compressing and recording high definition signals. In addition, some HDV cameras can record HDV on their own internal tape deck, but also have an HD-SDI output that can be fed to a record machine.

Some companies have created several HD recording formats and more are being developed. The current movement is toward "tapeless" recordings on optical disks, removable solid state media, and hard drives. Some experts are predicting the slow demise of videotape over the next few years.

Is HD Used for Film Production?

Yes, it is. Because high definition is capable of recording a large amount of visual information, it has been used in many feature films, including *Star Wars, Sin City, Collateral, Miami Vice,* and *Spy Kids.*

When high definition is used in productions intended for theatrical projection, the shooting frame rate is either 23.98 or a true 24 frames per second. There are several methods of recording HD for film and these vary according to the camera and recording methods available. The actual method of recording to HD is entirely dependent on the production's budget. It can range from recording HDV to high-end HD video tape machines, to recording a camera's output onto disk drives as data.

However, the answer to the question is yes, HD in a variety of forms is used for film production. The productions that have utilized HD vary from shorts to major studio film productions.

Are High Definition Images Always Used in the Digital Intermediate Process?

High def does not always enter the DI process, and HD is not the only way to obtain images for DI. Film is often used as a source for DI images, and an HD program may be onlined or conformed without ever entering a DI suite.

It is true that high definition images can be used for in the digital intermediate process. The digital intermediate process is for projects that are intended to be output to film. A high definition project that was digitally edited in a nonlinear editing system, and then output to a high definition video format, has not been through a digital intermediate process.

Doesn't Film Have More Resolution Than HD?

Yes, a 35 mm film frame has much more resolution than a frame of HD. A frame of non-anamorphically squeezed film is considered to have the equivalent of 4,000 lines of horizontal resolution, whereas 1080 is the horizontal resolution for the larger of the HD frames. However, usually a 35mm frame is exposed and in its original form as a 4 × 3 aspect ratio.

If the film image is not anamorphically squeezed, this 4 × 3 image is "cropped" at the top and bottom for theater projection or HD delivery. This cropping eliminates a great deal of the original image, and thus the size of the image used for the production is reduced by the cropping. In addition, a portion of a 35mm print is used for the optical (sound) tracks. The net result is that a frame of high definition still has much less resolution than the final frame of film, but the two are much closer than at first glance.

Isn't HD Just Like NTSC Only Wider and With More Detail?

Not really. High definition is a family of formats. Unlike NTSC, which is a single format with a single frame rate, HD has several frame rates and frame sizes.

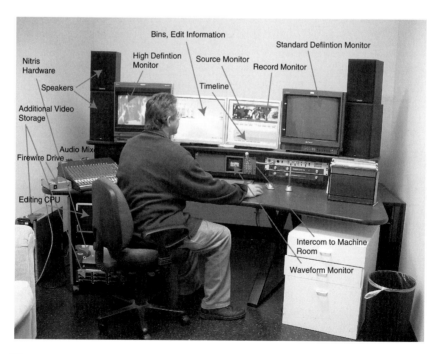

Figure 3.5 An online HD bay. This is an Avid Nitris online bay. With six terabytes of storage, it has the capability to store multiple shows without compressing the HD image.

The 12 high definition broadcast formats and over 50 production formats differ in many ways. If one does not shoot and edit in a compatible format with the show's delivery format, many expensive and visually unpleasant artifacts can be introduced into a project.

Is It True That a High Definition Frame Contains Much More Information Than an NTSC (Standard Definition) Frame?

Yes, the HD frame contains three to four times the visual information of the NTSC frame. That is why HD requires so much more powerful editors, larger hard drives, and faster computer processors than NTSC editing systems.

Is HD Going to Replace Film?

Yes, high definition video is going to replace film. There are many professionals who refuse to see the incredibly rapid inroads digital imaging has made into every facet of the visual industry. There are incredibly talented editors who still cut feature films using real film! But based on economics, image quality preservation, and the improvements in electronic equipment, coupled with the rapidly falling prices in HD, DI, and storage in a matter of years, digital images will surpass film in resolution, ease of use, and flexibility.

Of course, there will always be storytellers who choose to use film for their productions. Film, like black and white images, will have its place and continue to be used. However, in the long run, film will become a luxury rather than a necessity, and the professionals who know how to shoot and manipulate it will become fewer and fewer in number.

A similar process has occurred in the past. Decades ago, film was the primary source of daily television news footage. There were film labs in the stations and film editors cut the developed film, but

Figure 3.6 Sony CineAlta F900. The high image quality and film-like settings of the Sony CineAlta F900 make it a favorite for HD production. (Photo courtesy of Eyekandy Productions. Photo by Breht Gardner.)

video did not require developing, had sync sound and once technology was in place to edit these images, film production at local and national stations ceased to exist. Even commercials that had been shot and edited on film were delivered to television stations on videotape.

The same process is happening now. Film is physical, slow to process, and reaching the end of its evolution. The equipment that is used to manipulate it is fast being replaced by computers, and companies see the writing on the wall and are investing in digital image manipulation. Film is over. The reality is that economics have pushed DI and HD into the mainstream and film will be phased out as digital imaging solves its resolution issues.

Is HD Going to Replace SD?

Yes, and although it seems impossible, it will not take long. In 2009, digital broadcasting will replace analog frequencies. HDV will be over five years old. The excitement about HDV and HD is so pervasive among consumers, prosumers, and professionals, SD will become like black-and-white film and HD will become the norm.

With the introduction of low cost HDV cameras, decks and editors, along with mid-range HD cameras (like Sony's XDCAM HD), more productions are quickly moving into the high definition workflow.

Figure 3.7 Panasonic's AG-HVX200 has garnered a great deal of interest. It stores images and sound to solid state media.

Is HD the Best Format?

Not necessarily. Any production that is considering using high definition as an acquisition format must also factor in the final purpose of the production. High definition is not the a magic answer to every visual program. If one is considering the production of an in-house presentation or instructional video, NTSC might be a better choice when considering the life of the production and how the program is going to be viewed.

For some productions, film could be the preferred acquisition format. If a filmed program is destined to become a theatrical release, then the film could be electronically scanned and go through a digital intermediate process, totally circumventing any high definition production. The scanning of film into a digital intermediate format can result in much higher resolution than HD can provide. Currently, 4K is the highest common film scanning resolution. For a theatrical film release, it might be a better choice to shoot on film than in high definition, unless most of the film's images will be computer generated.

If all the production footage of a program already consists of standard definition footage, then a standard definition editing process might be the economically and practically preferred postproduction workflow. The end result would then be transferred to high definition for archiving.

Is Any HD Recording High Definition?

Not all recordings made to a high definition tape are high definition images. As with other formats, a low quality image can be recorded onto high definition tape. Consider an image played back from a VHS tape, blown up, and then recorded on a high definition tape. The tape is technically high definition, and the recorded image is defined as high definition, but the image on the HD tape is definitely going to be visually substandard, and no matter how many pixels it contains, it cannot be considered a true high definition image.

Or, consider shooting a scene with an expensive high definition camera where the signal from that camera is recorded on a top-of-the line high definition video recorder; however, the camera has a damaged or low quality lens. The recorded image will be totally flawed, but technically the video signal on the tape would be considered high definition.

In the early days of three-quarter-inch field production, a term called "broadcast quality" came to be used. This was a phrase that broadcasters used to aesthetically define the visual quality of a recording, but not necessarily its technical description. The video recorder has no way of knowing the quality of the signal it is being sent. It can only record the image quality available to it. Storing or recording an image onto a high definition format tape does not improve an image's quality.

Do Progressive Frames Have More Visual Quality Than Interlaced Frames?

There is no doubt that the progressive frame has more visual quality than an interlaced one. Even comparing the "smaller size" of a

Figure 3.8 VelocityHD is another choice in nonlinear editing systems.

720 progressive frame to a 1080 interlaced frame, the progressive frame wins, even with a stationary image where the two interlaced fields contain the same image degraded by interline flicker. This phenomenon, called the "Kell factor," reduces the perceived image to about 700 lines. Artifacts are more obvious with striped patterns that produce a "ringing" in the picture. These issues do not occur in a progressive image.

When movement is introduced, by the camera or the object, the difference becomes even more pronounced. Now there are two fields with half the resolution (350 lines when taking the Kell factor into account).

Progressive frames are easier for computers to process. However, as mentioned before, the final delivery frame size and frame rate are the most important considerations when choosing a high definition format. The ideal high definition production scenario is that of a single format, that being the same size, frame rate, and frame display as the delivery format.

If the final project's intended destination is to be output to film, there is no discussion. The production frame rate should be either a true 24 frames or NTSC-compatible 23.98 progressive frames. Many producers choose the 23.98 frame rate because it is NTSC compatible. In addition, it allows for easy outputs from the HD master to DVD, digital BetaCam, or even VHS.

There is one other issue concerning the progressive versus interlaced argument. When it comes to the actual viewing of progressive images, the receiver or monitor must be *capable* of displaying progressive images, otherwise the progressive is converted to an interlaced display for viewing. The good news is that the flat screens being sold today are progressive. The bad news is that some do not have the pixel count to accurately display an HD signal line for line. If you are interested in buying a flat screen, make sure to ask about the pixel count on the screen. Certainly these screens can display a high definition image, but in some cases, they do not have a full 1080 lines of resolution. As a result, the image is displayed with less than 1080 lines.

Will I Always Receive the Same High Definition Quality Images on My High Definition Television Set?

Unfortunately not, as digital broadcasting allows for additional compression with more signals. In other words, when an additional signal is broadcast alongside the station's high def signal, the high definition signal's quality is reduced to make room for the other signal.

Because the digital frequency for any station is limited, to add another data stream means something has to be sacrificed. In DTV, the high definition signal is compressed even more. A standard definition signal requires a data rate of between 4 and 7Mbps. This means three to six standard definition signals can be sent down a single DTV frequency. In the Los Angeles area, for example, there are more than a few stations broadcasting multiple standard definition channels on their digital frequencies along with their HD programming.

Chapter Three Summary

- Images shot in high definition can be viewed on a regular or "standard definition" television.

- There are several options for viewing the 16 × 9 high definition image on a 4 × 3 image ratio television set. One method is called "letterbox." Another is to eliminate a portion of the 16 × 9 frame at the sides. The act of selectively moving the wide screen image left and right for full screen viewing in 4 × 3 is called pan and scan. Many widescreen movies are still broadcast full frame, but most often the beginning and end are letterboxed because there is no way to pan and scan title or credits that reach across the screen. The third method of displaying 16 × 9 HD images in a 4 × 3 SD frame is to stretch the image vertically. This process is called 16 × 9 anamorphic, 16 × 9 stretched, or 16 × 9 enhanced.

- The ATSC DTV table was designed to satisfy many different needs of video and film users.

- The ability to broadcast the NTSC frame rates not only ensured a smooth transition to DTV, but the NTSC programs can also continue to be aired on the digital broadcast channels.

- United States consumers were so slow in replacing their working NTSC televisions with digital sets that the government delayed the handover of the analog television broadcast frequencies.

- The image you see from a digital broadcast is not always high definition.

- A digital TV is a digital format broadcast from an antenna, sent over the airwaves, and then received at the consumer's tuner. The tuner then converts the DTV signal and feeds it to the television screen.

- Many stations broadcast several programs on their digital frequency. A broadcaster can air five standard definition programs for one hour and then switch to a single high def program in the next.

- HDV is HD. It is recorded on a standard DV tape at a bit rate of 19Mbs for the 720 by 1280 progressive signal or 25Mbs for the 1080 × 1440 interlaced frame.

- Each manufacturer has developed particular methods of compressing and recording high definition signals.

- The current movement is toward "tapeless" recordings on DVDs, removable solid state media, and hard drives.

- Some experts are predicting the slow demise of videotape over the next few years.

- HD is used for film production.

- High def does not always enter the DI process.

- Film has a higher resolution than HD, by far.

- High definition is a family of formats.

- The best way to approach HD is to shoot and edit in a compatible format with the show's delivery format.

- The HD frame contains three to four times the visual information of the NTSC frame.

- High definition video is eventually going to replace film, in most cases.

- Film is physical, slow to process, and reaching the end of its evolution.

- HD is going to replace SD (standard definition).

- An HD recording is limited to the information provided.

- Progressive frames have more visual quality than interlaced frames.

- HD over-the-air compression varies according to how many signals the station is broadcasting on its frequency.

CHAPTER 4

More on the Technical Side

The high definition family of formats is complicated at first glance, but once one becomes used to the various options, it becomes friendlier and less challenging. When the dust settles and when analog broadcasting becomes a thing of the past, much of the confusion and technological nightmares will come to an end.

This chapter focuses on a few more of the technical issues related to high definition production and postproduction that are crucial to understanding the challenges of HD.

Frame Rates

Many productions prefer to shoot in 1080i59.94 because the majority of high definition broadcasters use this frame size and rate.

As mentioned earlier, ABC and ESPN chose 720p59.94, a progressive format, as their high definition broadcast standard. Due to the high amount of live sports programming these networks broadcast, their engineers felt that the 720p59.94 frame rate was the best choice for their productions.

Commercial producers shoot much of their original material on film and go through the same type of process. Once a 1080p23.98 master is made, versions of the program in other frame rates can be created through the used of the HD video tape deck. Depending on the model, a 1080p23.98 tape can be converted within the video tape deck and output to other formats.

If a producer is planning to deliver a program to be aired on ABC and ESPN, there will be different finishing requirements than for almost all the other networks. Most other HD content broadcasters want HD programs in 1080i59.94.

1080psf23.98

This is a "universal" format that can easily be converted to 1080i59.94 with the introduction of a 2:3 pulldown directly from the 23.98 final edited master. Another method of creating a 1080i59.94 master from 1080psf23.98 is to capture that original footage at 1080i54.94 and edit the entire program in a 1080i54.94 project. Many directors like the look of 23.98 even if the project is going to be delivered in 1080i.

1080psf23.98 uses less tape stock during production and less computer memory in postproduction because there are only 24 frames per second to store.

1080i59.94 (a.k.a. 1080i29.97)

Most HD broadcasters use this rate as their broadcast format. Conversions to NTSC standard definition are relatively easy. In addition, the look of 1080i is familiar to television viewers and the postproduction workflow is well established, as it was one of the earliest high definition frame rates used.

For a program that is intended for domestic use only with high definition generally 1080i59.94 is a perfectly acceptable frame rate. Syndication will most likely accept this frame rate in the future because it is easily compatible with standard definition NTSC, and the 1080i59.94 format is familiar with every HD content purchaser.

1080p24, 720p24, 720p23.98, and 1080psf23.98

These frame rates are used for several specific purposes. HD programs destined for film projection is one common use for these frame rates. Film runs at 24 fames per second, and these high definition frame rates can be transferred to film. If the purpose of shooting HD is to expose the video image to film, it makes no sense to shoot at higher frame rates.

The source of HD video for the creation of a film negative can come from a master videotape that has been edited and output to an HD tape. Another method of creating a film project using HD would be to utilize the Digital Intermediate process. The function of this procedure is to offline the program on a non-linear computer editing system using video dubs of the original footage, and then conform the high definition images in a digital intermediate suite. A video output from the offline session is used as a visual reference.

Another common use for these frame rates is for DVD production. Productions intending to be sold as progressive DVDs often use the 1080psf23.98 and the 720p23.98 as acquisition formats. Although 1080i59.94 may be a commonly used format, it is still an interlaced format.

Last, many prosumer cameras can shoot with one or more of these formats. Presentation projects, film festival projects, and some HD productions are shot on HDV. With inexpensive nonlinear editors able to handle these frame rates in HDV, shooting on HD becomes very cost effective.

720p59.94

As stated earlier, this frame rate was chosen by ESPN and ABC because they felt that the 59.94 frames of progressive images were more suited for sports programs, especially at ESPN, which is a sports network. There were other reasons, too, including the fact that progressive images are easier to edit, store, and manipulate. Also, the common artifacts associated with interlaced pictures do not occur in progressive formats.

Though the frame size of this format is smaller than the 1080 that most other networks use, there are nearly 60 full frames of information being presented per second. 1080i59.94, on the other hand, displays only half that amount.

1080psf29.97

Several production companies are looking at this format as an alternative to the 1080i59.94 format. The 1080psf29.97 frame rate somewhat resembles film because it is a progressive format with close to 24 frames per second.

1080psf29.97 offers some other interesting options. First, 1080psf29.97 is somewhat compatible with 1080i59.94. Several nonlinear editors view 1080psf29.97 as the same frame rate as 1080i59.94, and therefore it can be used in a 1080i59.94 project if the media is tape-based. This is done by telling the editor that the tape is 1080i when it is actually 1080psf29.97. This little trick does not always work with 1080p29.97 files, such as those created by the AG-HVX200 DVCPro HD, because these files are defined as a progressive format. Some nonlinear editors will not allow the mixing of progressive and interlaced files in a project.

If the project is in a 1080psf29.97 format, the output can be recorded to a 1080i59.94 tape, or a 1080i project can be recorded to a 1080psf29.97 tape. In both of these examples, the progressive frame is split in two and interlaced, but both of the fields are just an interlaced version of a single progressive frame, thus maintaining the progressive film look. However, it should be noted that there are four additional frames per second when compared to the 23.98p frame rate.

Integer Frame Rates

Other than the previously mentioned 24 frames per second, the remaining integer frame rates are rarely used because they are not directly or easily integrated into the NTSC 29.97 standard definition broadcast format. When the analog frequencies are returned to the government, currently scheduled for April 7, 2009, production companies and networks will probably start to use full integer frame rates for a portion of their programming.

Table 4.1 Data Rates of Uncompressed Standard and High Definition Video.

Width	Height	Frame Rate	Type	Mbps	GB per Hour
720	480	29.97	DV25	25	11
720	480	29.97	DV50	50	22
720	486	29.97	8-bit 4:2:2	168	74
720	486	29.97	10-bit 4:2:2	210	92
1280	720	23.97	8-bit 4:2:2	354	155
1280	720	23.97	10-bit 4:2:2	442	194
1280	720	25	8-bit 4:2:2	369	162
1280	720	25	10-bit 4:2:2	461	203
1280	720	29.97	8-bit 4:2:2	442	194
1280	720	29.97	10-bit 4:2:2	552	243
1280	720	50	8-bit 4:2:2	737	324
1280	720	50	10-bit 4:2:2	922	405
1280	720	59.94	8-bit 4:2:2	884	388
1280	720	59.94	10-bit 4:2:2	1105	486
1920	1080	23.976	8-bit 4:2:2	795	350
1920	1080	23.976	10-bit 4:2:2	994	437
1920	1080	25	8-bit 4:2:2	829	365
1920	1080	25	10-bit 4:2:2	1037	456
1920	1080	29.97	8-bit 4:2:2	994	437
1920	1080	29.97	10-bit 4:2:2	1243	546

There is quite a variation depending on how many frames per second and the size of those frames.

Mbps

Mbps stands for *millions of bits per second*, or *megabits* per second. It is a measure of *bandwidth:* the total information flow over a given time, or to be more specific, it is the measure of the number of bits per second.

Consider Mbps as the amount of information that is flowing through a pipe (although in real life, a data connection could be a wire or a wireless connection).

With a standard definition Digital BetaCam recording video at 8-bit YCbCr 4:2:2 and sampling in PAL (720 × 576) or NTSC (720 × 486) resolutions, compressed 2:1, its data "flows" through that pipe/wire at a bit rate of 90 Mbits/second, or 90 Mbps.

A high definition HDV signal at 1080i59.94 "flows" at 25Mbps. A 1080i59.94 HDCAM SR in standard quality recording HD at 4:4:4 "flows" at the rate of 440 Mbps.

> • In order for the video process to work properly, the data has to be able to flow from its source through all the wires, connections, and components to its destination. If these data pipelines do not have the bandwidth (or diameter if one is talking about actual pipes), the data just does not make it down the pipe. If a large amount of data is sent down a pipe that cannot accommodate the information, the same thing would happen as if a large amount of water was sent down a small pipe. A portion of water at the small opening will make it though, but whatever water cannot fit down the pipe at that moment will spill out at the head of the pipe. Whatever does not go down the pipe spills out and is lost. In terms of editing, the result is dropped frames.

Table 4.2 Data Rates of Compressed Video.

Tape Format	Record Mbps	HD/SD
HDCAM SR (SRW-5000)	4:2:2 = 444	HD
	4:4:4 = 888	
D1	270	SD
D5 HD	235	HD
HDCAM	140	HD
DVCPRO HD	100	HD
Digital BetaCam	90	SD
DVC PRO 50	50	SD
DVCAM, DVCPro, DV	25	SD
HDV 1080i	25	HD
DTV broadcasting (MPEG-2)	19.2	HD
HDV 720p	19	HD
BetaCamSX	18	SD

Note the large difference between HDV in this table and the 4:2:2 HDCAM SR recording in Table 4.1. The interesting aspect about compression is that if a format is half the data rate of another, it does not necessarily mean the image with the smaller data rate is necessarily half the visual quality. Each codec has its own properties.

To allow the data to flow, the HDCAM SR signal would require a bigger "pipe" than the HDV signal.

Throughput Needs

Let us assume there is a scene of video you want to record or play on a computer. The way the frames are created requires a certain amount of time to be transferred. The entire path these frames travel has to be able to deliver the images quickly. Otherwise, frames will be dropped or the image will freeze. So to view a high definition signal, not only does the computer disk have to be able to carry the data fast enough to deliver the information, but all of the wires and other devices that the image travels through must have that capability as well.

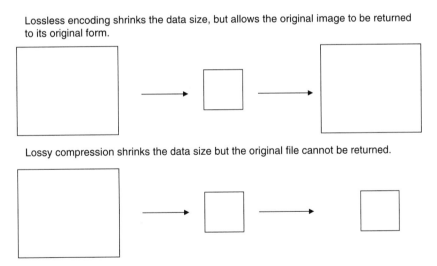

Lossless encoding shrinks the data size, but allows the original image to be returned to its original form.

Lossy compression shrinks the data size but the original file cannot be returned.

Figure 4.1 Lossless compression. Lossless is the preferred compression scheme. However, there are times when the product one is delivering determines how the compression works. Posting to the Web will almost always be a lossy compression process.

Compression, both through color subsampling and in overall data compression, allows an image to be recorded faster, requiring less tape and less space on a computer hard drive.

The data rates charts are similar. However, the first has to do with "pure" video frames with no compression. The second and third are specifications from manufacturers that include chroma subsampling compression and data compression.

In comparison, an uncompressed high definition data stream is 1.485 Gigabits per second. This amount of data is huge even by today's computer, film, DI, and television standards.

As discussed earlier, there are many different types of compression schemes that are designed to reduce the size of this data.

All Compressions Are Not Equal

As one looks though the compression ratios of different recording methods, it is interesting to note that not all compression schemes are equal. For instance, HDV compression is about 2.5 times as efficient as HDCAM compression. And the newer format, MPEG-4 AVC (also known as H.264), is twice as efficient as the MPEG-2 compression used for HDV. Sony and Panasonic have teamed up to use this codec for a non-tape-based disk recording format.

More Compression in Broadcasting

Even after the pristine HD master has been delivered, there is more compression on the way for the program within the high definition broadcasting path.

A program could be aired directly from the high data rate of an HDCAM SR, but the signal is immediately compressed to 45 Mbps because of the bandwidth limitation of Ku band satellites, which distribute the signal to the network affiliate stations.

The local station receives this data stream and processes it into a high definition signal for broadcast on its digital channel (DTV).

The station converts the downloaded satellite signal using an MPEG-2 encoder with a data rate output of 19.39 Mbps and then broadcasts it on its digital frequency. This is the signal that reaches the consumer's home from the station's antenna over the airwaves.

There are other ways high definition signals can reach an individual's home. The signal from the local network affiliate station is captured and delivered for either cable or satellite reception. Most consumers also want to see their local stations if they are on cable or satellite. One reason is that many of these consumers either cannot figure out how to get HD from over the air, or just do not want to invest in extra equipment.

No matter how the high definition signal reaches the consumer's television set, it is severely compressed. In other words, the high definition signal that is broadcast from an antenna to a home has a much smaller data rate compared to the original recorded video.

The six megahertz of bandwidth that the digital television stations are required to use for their DTV signals is quite large from a broadcast standpoint. A station can actually broadcast a high definition signal as well as other interactive information using this bandwidth. It is important to note that a station can choose to broadcast other information on that same DTV frequency. If other programs are broadcast on the same frequency as a high definition signal, the space available for that HD signal is reduced, and as a result, even more of the high definition information is compressed. Some stations do not air *any* HD signals on their DTV frequency and can then broadcast at least five separate NTSC standard definition channels. In Los Angles, the local NBC affiliate currently broadcasts its 1080i59.94 programming and its weather information on a separate channel. The local ABC affiliate, Channel 7, with more bandwidth available due to its smaller 720p59.97 HD signal, broadcasts its ABC cable news program and its local weather channel information on the same frequency as its HD programming.

Ultimately, it is obvious that the huge amount of data contained in a high definition image cannot be broadcast in its original state. This is why broadcasters, HD DVDs, cable operators, and satellite providers have to compress the high def images in

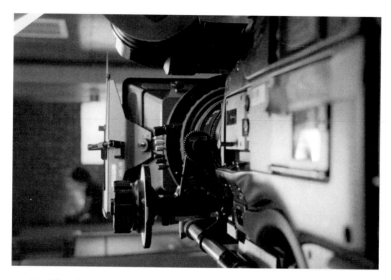

Figure 4.2 The Sony CineAlta F900 on set (Photo courtesy of Eyekandy Productions. Photo by Breht Gardner.)

order to get these huge images into our homes and onto our televisions.

Broadcast professionals know that this method of lowering the bit rate for airing does not yield the best visual quality considering how these images were originally shot, but at the present time, there is no better way to display them if one is to broadcast them. Certainly no American consumer, and probably no video or film professional, is going to purchase a professional VCR. That is what it would take to get compressed, high quality HD video on our television screens at home.

For a point of reference, the HD compression is far less destructive to the image compared to what happens to standard definition NTSC broadcasting.

Yet engineers are working on alternative compression schemes to improve the picture quality that reaches our homes. The amount of digital broadcasting space allocated to each station is finite. So, in order to get more image detail utilizing the same digital pipeline, compressing and decompressing this information has to improve.

Rapid Camera Development

Because the use and development of high def equipment is increasing rapidly, new cameras are being introduced with increased capabilities, frame rates, and better lenses almost monthly. Existing models are being upgraded and modified. Established postproduction paths are changing as these new and upgraded cameras, formats, and record decks with additional frame rate capabilities are being brought to the marketplace.

Analog equipment evolved slowly over the past 50 years. In contrast, digital equipment and processes are changing extremely fast. Announcements concerning upgrades and new equipment are happening almost monthly. With continuing hardware and software upgrades occurring very quickly, including the rapid advance of HDV, and the high definition workflow path changing so fast, it requires a current evaluation of the electronic landscape, which includes cameras, edit systems, and hardware accelerators.

The enticing aspects of HDV are twofold. Not only is the tape the same size at standard definition DV, the throughput of the signal is also low enough to work with existing firewire setups. Sony's

Figure 4.3 The interface to Apple's Final Cut Pro. Final Cut has become one of the leading editing systems, especially for those using Apple computers. (Photo courtesy of Apple Corporation.)

Table 4.3 Listing of Popular Editing Systems.

Company	Editing Systems	Effects Programs
Adobe	Premiere Pro	After Effects
Avid	Nitris DS, Nitris Symphony, Liquid, Composer Adrenaline HD, DV Express	Nitris DS
Apple	Final Cut Pro	Shake, Motion
Grass Valley	Edius	
Autodesk	Smoke, Fire, Flame, Inferno	Combustion
Leitch[2]	Velocity	
Artel	Media 100	
Pinnacle[1]	Studio	Hollywood FX
Quantel	eQ, iQ, sQ	Paint Box
Ulead	Videostudio	
Sony	XPRI, Vegas6	

[1]Owned by Avid.
[2]Owned by Harris Corporation.

This is a list of some popular editing systems. The cost of these software and software with hardware varies from $100 to several hundred thousand dollars. Of course, some of these programs require a computer, additional I/O equipment, and monitoring devices. Generally speaking, one could build a functioning high definition edit bay for about $30,000. HDV could be put together probably for about half that.

XDCAM HD records to optical disk and has several compression rates that it uses. Panasonic's AG-HVX200 DVCPRO HD P2 camera that records to solid state media can also record data flows at this low rate and some that are higher.

Editing Systems

The speed at which standard definition editing systems are adding HD and HDV capabilities is an indication of the growth of acceptance for high definition. As the capabilities, pricing, and added features to editing programs change monthly, it is a good idea to examine the current situations and concepts of the quickly evolving high definition workflow.

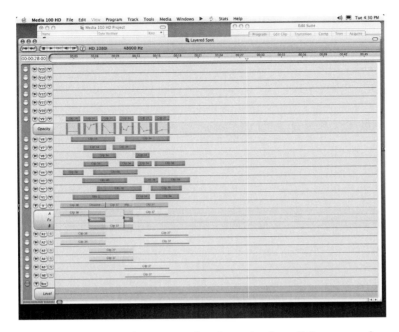

Figure 4.4 Media 100. This system has been in the editing arena for over a decade and has just upgraded its product to an HD system. (Photo courtesy of Media 100.)

Considering how editors, directors, and producers have preferences for their own familiar editing systems, here are some explanations of how the major editing systems work, highlighting their weaknesses and their strengths.

There are quite a few editors to choose from, and the price range is extremely wide. Sony Vegas is under $700, while a Symphony Nitris is over $50,000. Once one does acquire an editor, there are still monitors, scopes, and of course storage that need to be added to make the system viable.

Single Editor—Single System

The first situation to consider when planning a high definition post-production is how many editors and systems will be working on the project at any one time. If a project is being edited by a single editor, like an owner-operator, there are a number of cost effective ways to post high definition programs. As a matter of fact, the single-editor scenario is one of the simplest processes to examine.

In this configuration, there is no shared storage, and most often, there is no offline process. The original digitized footage is often used as the final product. Even if there is a low resolution approval version, usually the same system will be utilized to redigitize the necessary footage at high resolution for the final high resolution output.

There are a number of non-linear editors that can be used quite effectively for this type of postproduction. Adobe Premiere Pro, Avid Liquid, Canopus, Media 100, and Final Cut Pro are all cost effective and quite adequate for the challenge.

Medium-Scale Access and Post Challenges

In large-scale post facilities, shared media and multiple editors and editing systems become an issue. From a management standpoint, in large metropolitan areas there are many more editors familiar with the Avid family of editing systems. Again, the workflow for large-scale producers and productions requires seamless control of large amounts of media and often more than one editor working on the same project or segment. Avid and Apple have proven to be successful in sharing large amounts of data among multiple editing workstations. This is not to say that the other editing systems are not capable of multiple users/stations.

Program integration is another advantage when working with editing systems. Adobe has several products that integrate with its

Figure 4.5 Matrox is a manufacturer of video hardware. Its HD hardware integrates with Adobe's Premier Pro editing software. (Photo courtesy of Matrox.)

editing program (Premiere Pro). Adobe Photoshop, After Effects, Encore, and Audition are designed to be similar in their interfaces and work well together, and in some cases are connected to each other. Apple Corporation has its high-end editing program (Final Cut) that is also integrated with some of its other effects and sound programs (Soundtrack, Motion, DVD studio, Shake, etc.).

Hardware Acceleration

Besides the editing software, there is often additional hardware involved in the editing system. Some programs require the hardware to operate (like Autodesk's Fire and Quantel). Others use the hardware for input, output, editing codecs, and additional effects.

Grass Valley's Edius and most of Avid's product line have their own proprietary hardware. Autodesk and Quantel have dedicated hardware.

Several "third party" manufacturers have been very successful marketing input/output cards that, along with their software, provide additional power to some editing systems.

Two companies, Blackmagic Design and AJA Video Systems, have created computer cards that serve several functions for Windows and Mac computers. These boards first serve as input/output boards, but beyond the HD and SD capture functions, these products provide monitor output, machine control, and format conversions. In addition, these products come with thier own set of graphics and effects to enhance the operation of popular software-based editing programs like Premiere Pro and Final Cut.

Many editing systems make use of graphics cards that have preprogrammed effects and shapes. These graphics cards often have additional processing power built into their circuitry. This is the reason many editing software programs have specific requirements concerning the monitor display card that is used on the editorial computer.

One of the challenges many editors face is that it can be difficult, though not impossible, to offline edit on one brand of system, and online edit on another. There are software programs (like Automatic Duck) that translate from one program to another. It is also a matter of effects. A cuts-only program is fairly easy to convert from one

- There are quite a number of editing software products. Some can be augmented through the use of additional hardware manufactured by separate companies. Also, some of these programs have hardware accelerators that can improve the performance of the software. The hardware usually has preprogrammed effects that free up the computer to do other chores, speeding up the editing process.
- Each system has its own strengths and weaknesses, and there is a fairly large range of cost for each product. Some include software only and can cost up to several thousand dollars. Others use dedicated, priority hardware and can cost over $100,000.

program to another using the old edit decision list (EDL) format to transfer edit information. However, translation can be tricky when it comes to complicated picture-in-picture, blurring, or other very specific visual effects. Often the translation does not come across, and the effect has to be recreated. In a constant product environment, this added layer of software is not always advisable.

To be safe, it is best to keep things simple. Conform on the same brand and type of editing system that the creative editing was done on, and if possible, do not mix frame rates in a project.

Codecs

A big concern in any high definition workflow is the amount of computer storage that the project requires. This storage issue does not just concern the footage. Complicated effects need to be "rendered," meaning the computer has to create the effect as a new piece of media. This process not only takes up editorial/machine time, it also takes up more space on the computer's drives. Graphics, moving and still, consume additional hard drive space. One of the ways to save valuable space is by using sophisticated compression schemes called "codecs."

A codec has two similar definitions, but both mean the same thing: it is either an abbreviation for coder-decoder or for compressor/decompressor. The best codec is one that shrinks the amount of space needed for a file, while keeping the actual information intact. This is a lossless codec.

There are other codecs where after encoding, returning to the original quality is impossible. This type of compression codec is called lossy.

Saving space on hard drives is a concern for any HD project. DVCPRO HD, Apple Intermediate Codec, DNxHD, Blackmagic, Prospect HD, Aspect HD, and Connect HD are just a few of the codecs in use today.

Often codecs are used as the footage is being captured in a nonlinear editor. One reason is to save space on the editing system's hard drives and to put less strain on the editing system, as a smaller file is easier to manipulate. In many instances, codecs are used when capturing HDV. HDV was intended as a production format and although HDV can be captured and edited as MPEG-2, many editors prefer to capture the footage in a codec and use that file to edit

Figure 4.6 The linear bay of old still gets use as a dubbing and shot pull edit system. In a few cases, even for high definition, linear edit systems can be efficient.

with. Part of the reason for this decision is that it can be quicker and easier to render effects using the codec than the MPEG-2 file.

The downside of intermediate codecs is that they take up a lot more space than the original file.

Linear Online Editing

From 1950 to the early 1990s, video was edited by transferring images from one videotape to another. This form of editing, called

> • So many students and even beginning professionals forget the huge amount of work involved in the delivery aspect of a program. Not only does the show have to be shot, edited, and approved, there are also many mundane yet critical aspects of delivering a program to a client. Below is a short list of the considerations in the finishing and delivery of an HD (or any video format) program.
> Closed Captioning
> Blurring of all unwanted logos on shirts, hats, sweaters, etc.
> Blurring of license plates
> Dubs with labels
> Textless program with split audio (for foreign country sales/syndication)
> Licensing of music
> Protection dubs (when the client's original is lost)
> Quality Control (looking for analog or digital hits, film dirt or hair, video and chroma levels)
> Spelling check of lower thirds and credits
> All text within safe title
> All mattes match from one shot to another
> Approval dubs for client
> Delivering the program a week early for dubbing and closed captioning
> Licensing of stock footage
> It is obvious from this list why a visual program is expensive to produce and deliver. There are so many aspects that are not obvious to the viewer or novice. As one producer has said, "If it was easy, everyone would do it."

linear editing, was cumbersome and slow. In the mid- to late 1900s, linear editing was the most commonly used process of assembling a video show. As computers became more powerful, tape-to-tape editing became very limited in use and this process was delegated to making copies of video tapes, with small time adjustments, and creating clips from B-roll footage for feature films.

However, when HD arrived on the scene, the storage requirements for a long-form project were far too expensive for computer non-linear editing. Therefore, nonlinear HD editing was reserved for commercials (often seen during the Superbowl at halftime) and short-form projects. Longer TV movies, dramas, and sitcoms were finished the old-fashioned way: HD-to-HD tape editing in a linear bay. Hundreds of HD projects were finished using tape-to-tape editing systems pioneered in the late 1970s.

Even in 2004, the final year of Paramount Pictures' *Enterprise* was finished in a high definition linear bay. Effects and credit sequences

Figure 4.7 The quality control room is where the final edited video is examined frame by frame. Before a program is sent out, it is usually examined from start to finish to make sure everything is perfect from a technical perspective.

were delivered on HD, but since most of the transitions were cuts, it was natural to finish the program in a linear edit bay.

Chapter Four Summary

- Many productions shoot in 1080 frame size.

- The ABC and ESPN networks have chosen 720p at 59.97 frames per second as their high definition broadcast standard.

- Commercial producers shoot much of their original material on film and go through the same type of process. Once a 1080psf23.98 master is created, versions of the program in other frame rates can be created by a having the video deck convert the frame rate as it is playing.

- 1080psf23.98 (progressive segmented frame) is considered the universal format. This rate can easily be converted to 1080i59.94 with the introduction of a 2:3 pulldown directly from the edited master.

- This 23.98 frame rate uses less tape stock and less computer memory in postproduction.

- 1080i59.94 is a common frame rate because of its compatibility with the standard definition NTSC frame.

- The look of 1080i59.94 is familiar to television viewers, and the postproduction workflow is well established as it was one of the earliest high definition frame rates used.

- The disadvantage of the 1080i59.94 frame rate is that down-converting to 23.98 is expensive and causes some visual artifacts, the severity of which depends on how the conversion is accomplished and the nature of the original footage.

- 24 and 23.98 frames per second formats are used for programs that will eventually be exposed to and ultimately projected on film.

- 720p59.94 is the frame rate chosen by ESPN and ABC because their engineers and managers felt that the progressive images were more suited for the sports programs they produce. There were other reasons including the fact that progressive images are easier to edit, store, and manipulate.

- 1080psf29.97 (progressive segmented frame) has a film look because it is progressive.

- Mbps stands for millions of bits per second, or megabits per second. It is a measure of bandwidth, the total information flow over a given time.

- A high definition HDV signal at 1080i59.94 "flows" at 25Mbps.

- An HDCAM SR in standard quality recording HD in 4:4:4 "flows" at the rate of 880 Mbps.

- CCEC stands for constant communication and equipment check.

- Even if the program being aired comes directly from the high data rate of an HDCAM SR, the high definition signal is compressed to 45 Mbps to accommodate the bandwidth limitation of Ku band satellites, which distribute the signal to the network affiliate stations.

- The local station receives this data stream, and then converts the downloaded satellite signal using an MPEG-2 encoder with a data rate output of 19.39 Mbps.

- No matter how this high definition signal reaches the consumer's television set, it is compressed.

- If other programs are broadcast on the same frequency as a high definition signal, the space available for that HD signal is reduced.

- Single editor systems have fewer data sharing requirements than those that have multiple users and editing stations.

- Codec has two similar definitions, but both mean the same: it's either an abbreviation for coder-decoder or for compressor/decompressor.

- The best codec is one that shrinks the amount of space needed for a file, while keeping all the compressed information intact.

- There are many positions and jobs to do in the conforming of a visual program.

CHAPTER 5

Preparing for and Shooting in High Definition

The increasingly widespread acceptance of high definition has created some unique situations during production. Yet there are many production concepts used in standard definitions that carry over to the HD set.

Although many of the following suggestions and observations may seem obvious, they are only noted here because in the exciting and complicated environment of production, these issues are often forgotten.

Figure 5.1 Retail store. The decreasing price of flat screens has raised the public's awareness of HD, which in turn has increased the number of people who are watching HD productions.

Before diving into any details, it is a good idea to reiterate once again that the first rule of production for a high definition project is, if at all possible, keep the frame size and frame rate the same as the delivery rate. If this is not possible, the secondary protection plan is to definitely keep the frame rate the same as the delivery format. Several popular and high-end HD cameras shoot at only 720 by 1280. The upsizing to 1080 by 1920 is not that much of a reach; however, keeping the frame rates the same is the most critical aspect of avoiding costly conversion situations. The exception to this rule is 23.98psf, which can be converted to other frame rates without too much added expense or complication.

The Video Village

The cluster of electronic equipment on a set is often called a "video village." It is in this area where shots are replayed and examined for composition, focus, performance, color, and any number of concerns with a particular shot. I am not certain of the origin of the term, but considering the equipment, technicians, and people who end up hanging around the equipment, it is similar to a tiny centralized town.

Figure 5.2 Video village. The cluster of electronic monitoring equipment on a set is often referred to as the "video village." (Photo courtesy of Trygre Lode. Photo by Parlene Cypset.)

In some cases, there is also an editing system included either in the video village, or close by. As a reel of tape is finished, the footage is immediately captured, and the shots are cut into the scene to determine what kinds of additional footage might be needed.

Usually the equipment in the video village is not very mobile and is quite expensive. Although the video village is not for every production's budget or even shooting scheme, it has become more and more the safeguard against a slightly out-of-focus shot that could not be seen on a standard definition monitor.

Tube Versus Flat Screen

Most monitors that contain CRT (Cathode Ray Tubes) can only display an interlaced image. This is definitely not a good way to critically view a progressive signal, especially on set. If one is viewing progressive signals, the best way is on a high definition flatscreen monitor, shaded from the bright lights of the set and the sun. One should pay attention to the native dimensions of any flatscreen. There are 1920 × 1080 progressive displays available, although many are 1366 × 768. If this is the native dimension of a monitor, only the 720 image can be displayed pixel to pixel.

Standard Definition Protection Framing

Even though a program may be shot in high definition, often it will be viewed by the majority of the show's audience in a 4 × 3 standard definition environment. This situation occurs when a show is broadcast both in high definition and in NTSC standard definition. Most shows are still watched in standard definition. And even though a show might be shot, edited, and delivered in HD, all too often that show is down converted in full frame mode, which eliminates the sides of the HD image.

In the early days of high definition broadcasting, a comedian purposely placed visible action on the horizontal sides of the high definition frame, telling the audience that what was occurring at the far edges of the picture was only for those in the audience who had HD televisions. The standard definition audience could not see what was happening because their sets cut off the sides of the 16 × 9 image.

This situation of framing for standard definition television is hardly new to filmmakers. Directors and executives often consider the sides of the frame for NTSC 4 × 3 standard definition television broadcasts. Sometimes the program that is being shot on film is destined to be shown exclusively for television both in the United States and abroad; however, the original master is shot "4 × 3 safe," meaning that the program can be broadcast on standard definition television and only nonessential action occurs outside the 4 × 3 frame.

Many motion picture filmmakers choose to shoot "television coverage" for questionable scenes. In this way, the studio can alter the original feature film footage with the television coverage and still sell the film essentially with the same intent as for the movie theaters, but without the profanity or nudity.

Nonlinear editors, monitors, and viewfinders have 4 × 3 indicators to show which part of the image will be visible in a standard definition broadcast. In the production process, shooting for 4 × 3 when the frame is 16 × 9 is sometimes called "shoot 16:9 protect 4:3."

In Australia and the United Kingdom, there is a "protect 14:9" process. During production, all the essential action of the 16 × 9 image is kept within the 14:9 area of the 16 × 9 frame. In this way, when the 4 × 3 image is broadcast, it becomes a small letterbox (black margins at the top and bottom of the screen). This is a compromise between cutting off the sides of the frame, and having a totally letterboxed image shown in a 4 × 3 display.

Camera Lenses Are a Vital Aspect of Any Production

Anyone familiar with video or film production knows that lenses are as critical a part of the image capturing process as the camera itself. When considering renting a camera, one should also keep in mind the camera's ability to accept high quality lenses. The ability to choose styles and types of lenses is critical to many productions. Companies who make expensive HD cameras are always considering film productions as a market for their cameras, so lens interchangeability is a requirement.

Some HD cameras were designed with lens interchangeability from the beginning. There are also adapters available for the midrange cameras. Some HDV cameras have the ability to accept different types of lenses.

- One might think that shooting "television coverage" is redundant or even economically wasteful. However, there are many financial opportunities that film studios exploit in order to create additional revenue from their projects. There are many other opportunities to make money besides the theater box office for motion pictures. There are sales to the airlines and sales to foreign countries with different broadcast formats. Basic cable stations, broadcasts stations, and pay cable stations will pay for the right to air a movie, even long after it has left the movie theater. DVDs both as rentals and as purchases are very profitable for producers. Alternate shots and PG-13 line readings can often make a big difference in sales to these ancillary markets.
- There are cable programs that are made even when the producers know the broadcast license fee will not cover the production costs. However, sales of DVDs actually create more than enough money to generate a profit. In other words, the cable show is produced at a loss, but the program on the cable station acts as an advertisement for the DVD.

- Most live high definition sporting events are simultaneously broadcast in NTSC standard definition. It is fairly easy to tell when watching a high def broadcast if there is a concurrent SD broadcast because the HD graphics are placed far away from the edge of the screen. The graphics have been designed for a 4 × 3 image, but because the 16 × 9 high definition is so much wider, there is a noticeable gap between the edge of the graphics and the screen. Standard definition viewers do not see the gap because the sides of the HD image are cut off by the SD broadcast.

Editing HDV

With the high definition technology changing so fast, this subject may soon be a thing of the past. However, as issues have already surfaced regarding the editing of HDV, it will be discussed here.

There is a device called a Miranda that converts HDV MPEG-2 over FireWire to an HD-SDI signal. In addition, the Miranda has the ability to translate FireWire information into serial machine control.

When converting HDV to HD using a Miranda, an NLE can capture the original HDV media as full frame HD media. The advantage is that this frame is now full HD video and stays that way. The downside is that the editing system now requires a great deal of storage, which defeats much of the advantages of HDV. Yet even though this process can take up extra drive space, there is no GOP

Figure 5.3 The Sony HDV with a Miranda HDV to HSD-SDI converter. Although this combination converts the MPEG-2 HDV images to HD, it requires much more storage than importing and editing HDV natively in MPEG-2.

(group of pictures) to deal with, especially if the delivery format is HD. The entire post process is basically full frame, 1-to-1 HD.

HD 1080i59.94 Master With NTSC Media and a NTSC Delivery

NTSC standard definition footage is often mixed with high definition in an HD program. Many times this high definition master is destined for an NTSC broadcast. In some cases, the high definition version is simply a future protection master, not intended for broadcasting until a later date. However, blowing up standard definition footage and then down-converting that same footage back to NTSC severely compromises the original SD image. The time-consuming task of replacing the compromised footage with the original-sized NTSC, unaffected footage is one way to preserve the integrity of the standard definition version of this program. Or, to put it another way, some producers prefer to spend the time and extra effort to reedit the SD material back into the standard definition master.

Mixing SD (NTSC 29.97) With HD 23.98 Master NTSC 29.97 Delivery Frame Rate

When the high definition project is edited at a 23.98 frame rate, there is even more reason to reinsert standard definition footage back into a standard definition master. Many film studios and other producers create their HD masters in the "universal frame rate" to enable distribution in PAL or other frame rates or sizes. However, the conversion of 29.97 standard definition footage both in sizing and frame rates compromises the SD footage. Some producers will output a textless standard definition master so that the SD footage can be reinserted into the master and the titling can also be done in standard definition. This way the high definition program can be titled using the entire 16 × 9 screen, without having to keep the text inside the 4 × 3 safe title area necessary if the high def to standard def conversion was done simply as a video dub.

This separate treatment of the NTSC standard definition master will create additional expenses for the postproduction budget.

Table 5.1 List of Camcorders.
Below is a list of some HD camcorders, cameras, and record decks.

Manufacturer	Model Number	Format	Device	Notes
Panasonic	AG-HVX200	DVCPROHD	camcorder	
Panasonic	AJ-HX400	HD	camcorder	
Sony	HDW-750P	HDCAM	camcorder	
Sony	HDW-F900	HDCAM	camcorder	
JVC	GY-HD-100	HDV	camcorder	720p24, 720p30
Sony	HDR-FX1	HDV	camcorder	
Sony	HDR-HC1	HDV	camcorder	(prosumer)
JVC	JY-HD10U	HDV	camcorder	(to 720p, 30 frames per second)
Sony	HVR-ZE1	HDV	camcorder	
Panasonic	AJ-HDC27	DVCPROHD	camera	also known as Varicam
Canon	XL-H1	HDV	camera	
Sony	H-3	HDCAM	player	player
Panasonic	AJ-HD3700	D5	recorder	
Panasonic	AJ-HD1700	DVCPRO-HD	recorder	plays DVCAM, DVCPRO, & DVCPRO 50
Panasonic	AJHD-1200	DVCPRO-HD	recorder	
Sony	HDWF500	HDCAM	recorder	
Sony	HDW 2000	HDCAM	recorder	
Sony	HDW-S280	HDCAM	recorder	plays Betacam SP & SX
Sony	JH3	HDCAM	recorder	
Sony	SRW-5000	HDCAM SR	recorder	
Sony	SRW 5500	HDCAM SR	recorder	
Sony	SRW-1	HDCAM SR	recorder	portable
JVC	BR-HD50	HDV	recorder	
Sony	HDVR M10E	HDV	recorder	
Sony	HVR-M10E	HDV	recorder	

Tape Versus Optical Disk or Solid State Media

The transport mechanism for videotape within recorders and players requires a great deal of physical hardware to make a proper recording. Tape has to be loaded, tension between take-up and feed reels constantly corrected, and there are many moving parts that wear out. The newest technological advance in high definition cameras is that of using solid state memory, computer hard drives, or optical disks.

The Sony XDCAM not only records HD images onto an optical disk, it also records "proxy" images. Proxy images are smaller files that are identical to the original images, including picture, audio, and time code. Offline or creative editors can quickly transfer the smaller-sized proxy files for editing. Then when it comes to conforming, either the original XDCAM footage has already been transferred to the editing system, or the DVD disk can be used to batch digitize the necessary footage.

The Panasonic AG-HVX200 stores its various compressed standard definition and high definition video signals onto a solid state card. This media can be offloaded to a laptop or external hard drive and easily duplicated; however, at this point there is no smaller-sized proxy file available to be used with offline editing.

Solid state recording devices do not need the complicated moving parts that are in a tape-based camera. The camera's overall weight is lowered too, making the camera smaller and lighter. Although the solid state recording capability may lower the cost of the camera, usually this type of recording media is more expensive than videotape. There is also the additional challenge of what to do with the media.

This camera uses P2 flash media cards, actually a PCMCIA card, to store its 100 Mbps DVCPRO HD signal. There is also a hard drive outboard unit, but it cannot record 1080 size frames, only 720.

P2 cards allow for searching their contents through a navigation system on the camera's LCD screen for immediate playback. The cards

Figure 5.4 P2 card. The Panasonic AG-HVX200 stores media on a PIMCA card. The media can then be transferred to a laptop or external hard drive, or be played back. (Photo courtesy of Panasonic Electronics.)

come in 2-, 4-, and 8-gigabyte sizes. With P2 cards, there is no need to capture the media. The files can be downloaded to a nonlinear editing system or edited straight from the P2 card. The disadvantage of the P2 card is that although it is reusable, it is much more expensive than tape.

When a program that has used solid state camera media is finished and delivered, how does one archive the original production footage? Should it be played out onto videotape and stored? Should the files be transferred to a removable storage medium like a FireWire drive, or should the files be written to DVDs? This process increases labor and material costs, which has producers of large, tape-based productions that create hours of footage questioning their use of such a workflow.

Recording Media to Disk

The Sony XDCAM HD is designed to store its images on an optical disk. This camera design eliminates the need for videotape. The Sony XDCAM HD records its media on a blue laser optical disk, which eliminates the tape path in the camera. Rough edits can also be made in the camera, and footage can be organized in the field. Not only is the high definition footage stored on the disk,

Figure 5.5 DVCPRO P2 Store Drive. This device is designed to offload media from the Panasonic P2 PIMCA card. (Photo courtesy of Panasonic Electronics.)

there is also another, smaller video file with the same images, audio, and time code. These files, which are called "proxy files," can be directly imported into a nonlinear editing system. The XDCAM HD records at three different bit rates (18/25/35Mbps) using MPEG-2 media compression. In the spring of 2006, the CBS owned- and -operated stations (often referred to as O&O's) adopted the XDCAM HD format, intending to replace their digital BetaCam and BetaCam systems with the XDCAM HD format system.

Infinity Camera—Non-Tape Storage With Several Options

The Grass Valley Company, a subsidiary of the Thompson Group, has their own non-tape camera solution with their Infinity camera, which records its image to an Iomega REV cartridge, a FireWire drive, Compact Flash card, or even a USB stick. The modified Iomega cartridge disks allow users to record 45 minutes of high

Figure 5.6 XDCAM media. The Sony XDCAM stores its media on a rewritable optical disk, eliminating the need for complicated tape drives. The camera also stores a small image on the disk, called a proxy. These files can be imported more quickly to editors. When the program is done, the high resolution media can then be used for the conform.

definition video with complete flexibility in the use of encoding and compression schemes. Ideal for multi-format acquisition, as well as migration from SD to HD, the Infinity camcorder can produce several high definition formats: 1080i 50, 1080i 59.97, 720p 50, or 720p; 59.97, MPEG-2, or JPEG 2000.

Ikegami has a field pack that stores its high definition media from their HDN-X10 Editcam HD camera. Its images are recorded in full resolution on the FieldPak2 removable media with the Avid DNxHD codec in MXF file format. This is the same codec that was adopted by the American Idol production company in order to save drive space.

Another solution is to have hard drives to externally record the camera's media. Two such devices are Focus Enhancements and

Figure 5.7 Infinity camera. Thomson's new Infinity camera stores its media onto either removable storage or solid state memory. It also can be connected to a network via a gigabit ethernet. (Photo courtesy of Thomson Grass Valley.)

Wafian hard drives. Wafian's hard drive uses CineForms' wavelet compression codec. This allows the resulting data to be used immediately in Adobe's Premier Pro.

For Final Cut Pro, Avid, and other computer editors, the media has to be converted (transcoded) first in order to be used. Focus Enhancements' devices convert FireWire drives into a digital disk recorder (DDR).

Again, as more and more productions dive into high definition production, there will be additional equipment, both for production and for editing.

Delivery Requirements

The determination of final delivery format for any high definition program is the very first question that must be asked and hopefully answered before production starts. If the answer is unclear or unknown, the "safest" choice is to shoot at 1080psf at 23.98 frames per second.

Mixing formats can be challenging, but if original production footage is shot in the correct frame rate, then the small portions of the program can be converted to the editing and/or output frame rate. There are also some NLEs that allow mixing a large number of frame rates in a single timeline. Each editing system has its own particular way of dealing with the non-native rates. In addition, some require rendering or manually changing the clip's speed or other adjustments. It is a good idea to do tests on these conversions and workflows early in the production to see if the results are acceptable. In fact, some postproduction companies will do these short tests at no charge in hopes of capturing the business of the entire production.

There are two suggestions for any HD production:

1. Test everything. Make sure the frame rate, color, camera look, and editing system work.
2. Do not mix codecs, frame rates, or frame sizes if it is avoidable.

Motion Effects and Alternative Frame Rates/ Sizes—Change Tapes

Some slow-motion effects can be achieved by shooting at differing frame rates, and then converting the footage in your nonlinear editor. You can shoot several different frame rates, then add that footage to the time line and adjust its speed. There are also times during the production process when different frame rates are used for a specific effect or look.

If at all possible, each production tape should only have a single frame rate recorded on it. If you are planning on shooting at a different frame rate to be slowed later, a new tape with the different frame rate should be used, and clearly labeled as such. If these changes are known in advance, the reels should be pre-labeled.

23.98 is Not 24; 29.97 is Not 30 But Could Be 59.94i or 29.97p

Many high definition problems stem from people being afraid of telling the truth. Sales and marketing people like to talk about and sell 30-, 60-, and 24-frame production cameras when they are really talking about cameras that shoot at 29.97, 59.94, and 23.98 frames per second. To add more confusion, there is a true 24 frames per second frame rate (used for film production). There are also cameras that can record 30 frames per second, but most productions use the NTSC-compatible 29.97 frame rate.

This asterisk mentality (look at camera rates of integers with an asterisk, and in the fine print, it often says it is in a fractional frame rate, compatible with NTSC) has caused much head scratching for those new to high definition.

Many professionals and sales people, in their attempt not to confuse the public, "round up" their frame rates, which only causes more confusion. A production intending on going to film will shoot at a true 24 frames per second, yet a behind-the-scenes featurette might shoot at 23.98. In the "rounding up" world, both of these frame rates would be 24, which is not true at all.

Likewise, 29.97 frames per second is not 30. But 29.97i is the same as 59.94i and can be mistakenly also referred to as 60i. However, there is a 59.94i as well as an integer frame rate of 60i. The only current use for integer frame rates is for a production heading to film.

Camera and Record Deck Consideration—Testing and Monitoring

Even if the crew has extensive high definition experience, it is always a good idea to revisit the technical aspects of the high def equipment, postproduction, and delivery landscape. Now that high def has become mainstream, manufacturers are releasing new versions of existing equipment along with totally new record decks, editors, cameras, and camcorders.

Keeping Updated Via Email

There are several excellent resources that are free to sign up for to keep abreast of breaking news in the HD world. Millimeter, DV, High Def, Video Systems, Creative Cow, and High Def Forum are just a few of the online resources that are available. Some of these sites produce monthly newsletters that are delivered via email. Timely and well written if one is interested in current HD information, these are excellent ways to keep up with the changes that are occurring.

- In 1965, Gordon Moore, co-founder of Intel, the world-renowned chip maker, noticed that the number of transistors in a square inch on an integrated circuit had doubled every year since the device had been invented. Moore then made a prediction that that trend would continue for the foreseeable future. Although the pace slowed a bit, data density has indeed doubled approximately every 18 months.
- Along with this 18-month doubling of data density, the drive capacity and speed of processing and data transmission have resulted in astounding changes in HD production techniques and technology.
- Applying this to the producing of an HD project, it is always a good idea to check on the latest available technology being used in the HD world. Unlike older analog technology, which took decades to develop, today's cameras, record decks, codecs, and editing systems are being revised and upgraded almost monthly.

Editorial Equipment Consideration

How a program is going to be edited is often a decision that needs to be made by the production company or the already-hired editor before production starts—especially if HDV or alternative frame rates (29.97psf, 30, 60, etc.) are going to be used.

It is a good idea to check the current editing opportunities. There are many updates and new versions of editing software, and it is only smart to be current with patches, updates, and minimal cost downloads.

Editing a show with a product that is no longer being supported by the manufacturer because of an editor's fondness for a certain interface can be a financial and technological mistake. With so many new codecs being introduced, there can be some great advantages to simply upgrading editing software. This is especially true with HDV. One should always check about current drivers for controlling any cameras as well as updates to editing software.

Tape Labeling in the Field

Because there are so many high definition variations, it is important to label tapes properly with the following:

Date
Frame size
Frame rate
Shooting speed
Color sampling
Director
Production Name
Location

Not only does the tape need to be labeled properly, the record deck and camera also need to be checked at regular intervals to make sure the equipment is in the correct situation (CCEC). A power surge or change in camera location can potentially inadvertently alter a camera or record deck's settings. It is also a good idea to notate and store specific settings in a log book so that if something is changed or lost, the settings can be quickly restored. Many cameras and record decks have the ability to store their current setting. Decks with a particular color sampling cannot play back alternative sampling. It is a good to notate the sampling rate (X:X:X) on the tape to avoid miscommunication and bad offline dubs.

Audio Concerns

It is a well-known fact that an audience relates sound to picture. In other words, given two identical projects, one with a great sound track and the other with a poorly mixed one with few effects and so forth, the audience will actually think they are seeing a better "picture" when hearing the superior audio. Audio, from location shooting to sound design to mixing, is an often overlooked portion of a program.

For example, there really is no such thing as a silent location or stage. Every room or location has is own unique sound. To help the audio team, recording 30 seconds to a minute of ambience at a location, along with an audible and visual slate, can save time in the editing room and improve the sound and therefore the look of a program.

Heads and Tails

There is always a chance of a time code break when starting a scene. It is a good practice to wait 5 to 10 seconds at the beginning of the scene before calling for action. And it is likewise a good practice to wait a moment or two when the scene has stopped before calling "cut."

Makeup

The high definition image contains great amount of visual detail. There are even some motion picture film performers who refuse to perform in high definition because they feel it is "too real"; actually, they are saying high definition video is "too realistic."

Whereas film "softens" reality, high definition video without extensive light expertise comes across looking harsh, often with severe shadows. This is not the environment that actors and actresses want to be seen in. They want favorable, flattering lighting. It is important to have a makeup artist and lighting director/director of photography who understand the needs of film actors and their wants in the new world of high definition.

Slates, Tape Logs, Clapsticks

There should always be an individual on the set taking notes. These notes can be taken in several formats. Sitcoms and single-camera

Figure 5.8 Clapsticks. Clapsticks like this one are inexpensive, but provide invaluable information about the scene and take, and if problems arise can even be used to sync up audio and video.

dramas often use scripts to indicate reels, cameras, and time code and scene notations. This information, cross-referenced in a book, is very helpful when it comes to the editorial process.

In documentary productions, different types of reel identification plans are used, often revolving around subject, date, and location. This information input into a database or spreadsheet can then be examined in many different ways. Ultimately, footage organization is vital to the completion of any visual program, from a school project to a feature film.

Slating

If shots are intended to be without sound, they still should be slated. A visual reference is always helpful when logging and organizing footage. Some cinematographers and directors prefer that the slate be recorded prior to the beginning of the shot. This avoids interfering with the actors or flow of the shot and facilitates the complicated aspect of keeping focus on the action.

If there is time, it is also a good idea to "tail slate" each shot. A tail slate is recorded at the end of the shot with the slate upside down. This is a safety action to protect against the possibility that the video deck or camera operator has not gotten the machine into record when instructed and the slate has not been recorded.

Clapsticks

Clapsticks actually have a very important role in productions. Not only do they provide slate in formation, they have been used for half a century to sync audio. Although videotape has eliminated much of the sound syncing problems, when audio is being recorded on a digital audio tape (DAT) or another recording medium besides the cameras', audible slates as well as some sound reference that is on both the video and the audio sources are vital. In a recent student production, this process was forgotten in the rush to finish the project, and an entire day was spent locating and syncing the dialogue with the correct shot.

Lighting

Lighting, like audio, is critically important to the look, feel, and final result of the production. One of the reasons it takes so much time to set up a feature film shot is that directors and producers know the power of lighting a set correctly. Other than the frame rate, lighting can have the most dramatic impact on how a program looks and ultimately feels.

An experienced high definition lighting director working alongside a knowledgeable high definition director of photography can make a show that much more impressive through the use of creative lighting, but it does take up precious production time.

Camera Movement

Camera movement adds a special visual interest to any shot or scene. There are many ways of achieving camera movement without hindering the production process. Small dollies, manual cranes, and the use of a Steadicam™ are affordable for almost any production, and should be considered in shot selection. One must be aware of the production's frame rate. Rapid movement in a 23.98 frame rate can cause the appearance of strobing.

23.98 Speed of Camera Movement

23.98 has far fewer (less than half) images of a 59.94i frame rate. This issue is of vital importance when considering horizontal frame movement. Directors, Directors of Photography (DPs), and camera operators who are used to operating in standard definition, or HD at 29.97i (59.94), may have to consider slowing down horizontal camera movement. Better yet, it is a good idea to consult with other film camera operators because of the few frames per second in this frame rate.

Professionals who work in film production know about the horizontal movement of the camera or object. With only 24 individual frames per second, a quick horizontal movement can ruin a shot. Therefore, horizontal movement, whether it is camera or actor, should be kept to a minimum. Otherwise that movement, rather than resulting in a pan of quick motion, can result in an image that is just a series of individual frames.

HD record decks (those that are separate from the camera) have multiple audio channels. Even if you are planning to record audio on a separate system (DEVAS, DA88, DAT, etc.), it is prudent to split off the feeds and also send them to the video record machine. This provides excellent protection, recording the audio at the same frame rate as the video and in sync with the picture.

There have been problems with double system recording when the outboard audio recorder has not been properly synced with the frame rate of the production. For lower budget productions, this multiple track availability can eliminate the need for a spare audio recording device.

- The frame rate of 23.98 poses its own set of issues. Here is how one sound professional handled his own 23.98 production. The show was shot in 23.98, and edited in the same frame rate.

  "The Cameras were Sony 900's running at 23.976P (23.98 rounded up) mode and the sound recorders were a brand name, Deva 5 and a Deva 4. We ran Time of Day time code on all cameras as well as on the Deva sound recorders. The time code was derived from Ambient Tri Level Sync Lockit Boxes, and we attached one to each camera plus one from which I split the OP between the two Deva recorders. I calibrated the ambient master controller against GPS time the night before the shoot, and then calibrated all of the Lockit boxes against the controller on the morning of the shoot.

  Time code was Time of Day (TOD) and user bits (UBITS) were set to read camera number and roll number, i.e., camera 1 roll 3 would be UBITs 10000003, and camera 3 roll 5 would read UBITs 30000005. Sound UBITS read just a roll number, so roll 4 was UBITS 00000004. Audio was recorded onto the Devas at 48 kHz, 23.976 frames per second.

  We did run a Time Code (TC) slate on the day, but owing to a bit of a rush just before we started shooting, I was unable to update the TC on the slate so it was reading a little out and would not in fact have been of much help in syncing up—other than the clapper stick bits! Note to self: don't make this mistake again.

  Audio track allocations were as per various emails and transatlantic conversations that were had prior to the shoot, but basically we put a personal microphone on everyone involved and recorded each contributor to a separate track on one Deva or the other. An "on the fly" mix was made which was recorded to each video camera and onto one of the Devas. Audio files were recorded to the hard disk drives of the Devas, and then mirrored off to DVD-RAM disks. The files were mirrored as FAT 32, 24bit mono wav files.

  In terms of getting the talent microphones, the original plan was to use wired lavs for Richard and the actors, and radio microphones for the competition winners. In reality we had so much interference on the cables from dimmed lights and other sources that we used wireless microphones for all of the participants."

Time of Day Versus Continuous Run Time Code

Time of Day (TOD) time code seems cool and can be used for multiple camera situations. For most productions uses, however, continuous time code is much more desirable. TOD time code automatically creates a time code break once the take is over. Broken time code can cause problems during the editing process. If you batch capture a tape, the edit software may not recognize a clip with time code errors, and it can cause time and expense in the final online conform. An excellent use for time of day code would be for a concert or live performance being taped. With TOD code, cameras and audio tracks can be synced easily.

Some productions use both Time of Day and continuous time code. In this process, continuous time code is recorded on the time code track, while time of day is recorded on the audio track. In post-production, the window dubs can have both codes burned into the picture, facilitating the syncing of the different cameras.

Graphics

It is important to make sure you are communicating with your graphics designers as to your frame rate and frame size (CCEC). It is always a good idea to get a test graphic and examine it before assuming that all the graphics will be perfect. There are too many variables in HD to assume anything will work the first time. Frame rates, frame sizes, interlaced versus progressive, RGB or "601"video colors—these are all issues that need to be discussed. It can take quite a long time to render HD graphics, so if you have graphics created in low resolution for offline editing, remember to have these graphics rerendered in HD for the online conform before the session starts.

Delivery Issues

Knowing the final delivery specification is vital to any high definition project. Different broadcast companies have different delivery specifications. When it comes to high definition DVD delivery, each company has its own requirements which change, depending on the project. Common DVD delivery rates are 1080psf23.98, 1080p29.97, and 1080i59.94.

- An Avid solution to making an alternate frame rate:
- Using the Timewarp effect—part of the FluidMotion effects engine in Media Composer Adrenaline HD and Avid Xpress Pro HD—the user can create alternate frame rates and keep the original audio in sync.
- The Timewarp effect can be used to create all the frame rate conversions needed. The list below gives the necessary values needed to create any frame rate.

1. Create 29.97 NTSC project.
2. Capture shot to be converted.
3. Edit onto timeline (V and A).
4. Apply the Timewarp effect from the effects palette.
5. Select FluidMotion from the "Render Using" menu.
6. From the Formats menu, select Interlace as input and Progressive as output.
7. Open the Speed graph and enter 125 into value entry box at the bottom of the window.
8. Render.

- The result will be a progressive clip of the same duration but now running 125% faster. When this clip is imported back into a 23.98p project, it will be slowed down by 25% due to the 1:21 frame relationship. This way, durations remain the same and the original audio remains in sync.
- In order to get the clip back into a 23.98p project, export V only as a QuickTime reference and the audio as a WAVE file.
- Import these two files back into a 23.98p project and sync the V-only clip with the A-only clip using AutoSync. The result is a sync VA clip in a 23.98 frame progressive format.
- When importing the QuickTime file into the 24p project in either Media Composer Adrenaline HD or Avid Xpress Pro HD, the user may see a message indicating that the source is interlaced in a progressive project. Click OK and continue.

Known, current delivery specifications for the networks include the following:

ABC, FOX, ESPN: 720p59.94

CBS, NBC: 1080i59.94

Dolby 5.1

Another exciting aspect of high definition is the ability to record and broadcast Dolby 5.1 surround sound. With five separate speaker locations and a subwoofer channel, Dolby 5.1 brings theater-style audio to the HD experience. However, it should be noted that not all stereo mixing boards or systems are capable of separating out these signals and encoding them.

Again, as a preproduction chore, it is a good idea to explore the sound capabilities of the intended audio facility to determine if they really meet the needs of a high definition production. This includes being able to play and record to the specific HD tape format that the show will be finished on.

Chapter Five Summary

- CRT monitors are interlaced.

- In some cases there is an editing system on set.

- Many programs, even though they are shot in high definition, will be viewed by the majority of the show's audience in a 4 × 3 standard definition environment.

- It is important to remember that the sides of the 16 × 9 frame will not be seen in the 4 × 3 monitor unless the image is letter-boxed.

- Many motion picture filmmakers choose to shoot "television coverage" for questionable scenes. In this way, the studio can alter the original feature film footage with the television converge and still sell the film essentially with the same intent as for the movie theaters, but without the profanity or nudity.

- Many NLEs, monitors, and viewfinders have 4 × 3 indicators to show which part of the image will be visible in a standard definition broadcast. In the production process, shooting for 4 × 3 when the frame is 16 × 9 is called "shoot 16:9 protect 4:3."

- It is easy to tell on the high definition side if there is a concurrent SD broadcast because all of the graphics are placed far away from the edge of the HD screen.

- Camera lenses are a vital aspect of any production.

- The Miranda is a device that converts HDV MPEG-2 over FireWire to an HD-SDI signal.

- In many NLEs, there is an additional option to reduce that data rate to its own intermediate codec.

- The Sony XDCAM not only records HD images, it also records "proxy" images. The newest technological jump in high definition cameras is that of using solid state memory, DVDs, or mini DVD cassettes to store data.

- Mixing formats can be challenging, but if original production footage is shot in the correct frame rate, then the other small portions of the program can be converted to the editing and/or output frame rate.

- If at all possible, one should not mix frame rates on the physical production tape.

- 23.98 is not 24; 29.97 is not 30 but could be 59.94i or 29.97p

- Complete tape labeling in the field is a necessity.

- It is a good practice to wait 5 to 10 seconds at the beginning of the scene before calling for action. It is also a good practice to wait a moment or two when the scene has stopped before calling "cut."

- Lighting, like audio, is critically important to the look, feel, and final result of the production phase.

- Camera movement adds a special visual interest to any shot or scene.

- 23.98 has far fewer (less than half) images than a 59.94i frame rate. Restrict camera and subject movement when shooting at this frame rate.

- Make sure you are communicating with your graphics designers about your frame rate and frame size (CCEC).

CHAPTER 6

Real Postproduction Paths

High definition is used in a wide range of broadcast and non-broadcast situations. Its high quality makes it a perfect production medium for presentations that are projected on widescreen venues as well as DTV HD broadcasts. High definition is used for all sizes and types of film projects, from small student presentations to big-budget feature films; probably most obvious, high def is used by producers who create programming for cable, broadcasting, and satellite networks.

The following examples are real productions that have occurred in the high definition space.

That Guy

HD Shoot, HD Edit, HD Finish

That Guy is a 10-minute high definition short, which was produced as a talent showcase for the participants. It is a perfect example of a high definition show that ran smoothly, even though there were green screens and smaller effects. As explained below, there were two different frame rates and sizes used within the project.

It took nearly two years from the first script meeting to the final HD conformed delivery. The camera used was a Sony CineAlta F900. This is a top-of-the-line, high definition camera that has been used in many high budget film productions, including *Star Wars* and *Collateral*. Because this was a showcase production, the producers knew that multiple presentation formats could potentially be needed, including down-converting the program to DVD, NTSC, HVD, and possibly even PAL, which is why they chose to shoot at a frame rate of 23.98.

There were no previs (pre-visualization) sessions or storyboards created to plan the shots. Although there were four days planned for production, an extra day was needed to shoot pickups. There is no way to tell if storyboards or a previs would have saved that extra day of shooting. It was to the production's advantage that several of the crew members had already worked on high definition projects.

The shooting took place in Hollywood, California. The original camera footage was shot on Sony HDCAM stock, and then dubbed to Panasonic D5 stock. It was decided to dub the HDCAM footage to D5 because the original HDCAM footage had a large number of

Figure 6.1 Still from *That Guy*. Because of its cost-effectiveness, the high definition format is being used more and more to create shorts to be entered in film festivals and to provide a showcase for actors, directors, cameramen, etc. Note that the brand name of the soda was blurred. The majority of the footage in *That Guy* was shot in high definition at 1080psf23.98 in an 8-bit depth. (Courtesy of Eyekandy Productions. Photo by Breht Gardner.)

time code breaks. The postproduction team decided that these code breaks would cause postproduction capture problems, so the five HDCAM reels were dubbed across to fresh stock with continuous time code. The choice of D5 for the dub was made because, at the time, the editing house only had two high definition machines, an HDCAM and a D5.

The new D5 master was dubbed once again, this time to Sony DVCAM standard definition tape. These tapes were used for the creative editing process. During the transfer to DVCAM, a "burn in" of the 29.97 and 23.98 frame rates was recorded into the DVCAM visually.

The offline editing session was done using Avid Express Pro v.4 software on a Macintosh G5 computer. The frame rate was an NTSC standard definition rate at 29.97 frames per second. The file that was output for the finishing facility was a 23.98 frame AAF (Advanced Authoring Format). The AAF file was used to conform the high def footage into the final master. A QuickTime output was also sent to the finishing facility as a visual reference.

The dubs, down-conversions, and high def conform were all done at New Wave Entertainment and overseen by Jonathon Freeman and Breht Gardner.

Green screens were used for the several composites. Editor Mike Wolf used Adobe After Effects v.6.5 Professional (production bundle) for the compositing work. The software program used within After Effects to create the composite was a "Primatte" Keyer.

In a production, the choice of green screen or blue screen is dependent on several factors. The first is which colors the subject being shot contains. If an actor has blue eyes, it would be wise to use a green screen. The second consideration is what subject is being keyed over. If the subject is supposed to be in a green forest, using a green screen can hide some keying flaws. In the case of *That Guy*, the bar scene, where most of the program takes place, had a great number of blue lights. So, using a green screen for the television composite was the logical choice.

Figure 6.2 Green screen. The green of the television monitor was replaced with a standard definition edited video. Note the tracking marks at the top left and right of the television screen. Nonlinear editors usually have tracking software so as to program keys to use the same movement that is occurring on the screen. The tracking marks make it very easy to follow a moving object, like those used in green screen effects. (Courtesy of Eyekandy Productions. Photo by Breht Gardner.)

The green screen composites were output to a QuickTime file and edited into the offline file to ensure continuity. These files were also provided in high definition on a DVD to the finishing facility. Another effect was to simulate the POV (point of view) of looking through a digital camera. Simple but effective, this was a circle and a vertical matte created in Photoshop. This image, along with its accompanying "hold out" or "matte," was used to cut out the picture. It too was provided as a file to the finishing facility.

An Avid Nitris DS was used to conform the movie. (This is a different software program than the Avid Symphony Nitris). The AAF file was emailed to the finishing facility. This file contained all the information for the video conform, including the opening credits. The D5 footage was captured at full uncompressed resolution. As mentioned earlier, the composites and end titles were provided on computer files.

Few issues were encountered during the conform process. Most of the following adjustments are common in the finishing process of a project similar to this one.

The project was shot in 16 × 9 high definition, but was always planned to be matted in a narrower format. During the editing process, a 2:35 matte was added. Titles had to be slightly adjusted as the translation from the offline editor to the finishing computer did not come across in the same positions. In addition, small vertical adjustments were made to some of the DV footage as it was shot full frame 4 × 3. This frame format allowed for some creativity in the vertical placement of the 4 × 3 image behind the 2:35 matte. The title crawl was eliminated with 23.98, but jitter problems came into play. In order to eliminate that jitter, the crawl either had to be reduced significantly in size or the speed of the crawl had to be slowed so much that it was unacceptable. Single cards were chosen as an alterative and worked much better with the beat of the end music.

The producers of *That Guy* had always intended to make standard definition NTSC copies of the finished production as a letterboxed copy. In this way, there would be no conversion issues in SD, and the entire program could be seen in a 4 × 3 monitor.

Figure 6.3 Green screen effect. This is another example of a green screen effect in the short *That Guy*. The center of the screen has been replaced by a graphic. (Courtesy of Eyekandy Productions. Photo by Breht Gardner.)

Once all the text and 4 × 3 footage were adjusted, a textless, unmatted program was output to D5. The textless version was color timed using a tape-to-tape process. The color corrector was a DaVinci 2K. The product of this session was a new, color corrected D5 master. The color corrected master was then captured back into the Avid Nitris DS. This single piece of "color timed" media was placed on the Nitris' timeline. Titles and end credits were then given a final check.

Because the color corrected version of the production was textless and unmatted, its vertical placement behind the matte could still be adjusted. It is always a good idea to not put any effects, including mattes, in an output for color correction. This way the footage is colored, and as a result, adjustments to effects, mattes, and so forth can still be made to the color timed media that is returned to the editing system.

Once titles and picture were double-checked, finalized, and approved, another D5 version was output from the nonlinear Avid Nitris DS. This master, still in HD at a frame rate of 1080psf23.98, was the final product of the finishing process. This master can be played out of the D5 machine in a variety of formats, including, but not limited to, NTSC standard definition full frame, NTSC letter-boxed, PAL, and 1080i59.94. For protection, and in case there was a need to make changes in titles, a textless color corrected version of the show was also output to the same D5 tape.

Figure 6.4 *That Guy* titles. Non linear editors have a great deal of capability. Most can do blur effects, titles, and sophisticated color correction. (Courtesy of Eyekandy Productions. Photo by Breht Gardner.)

That Guy was mixed on another Avid Product: Protools HD. The entire audio track was delivered on a DVD data disk as an OMF Avid audio format. This stereo, mixed track was married to the picture in a matter of minutes using a Fairlight audio bay and laid back to the 23.98 D5 master.

Super Bowl Feature Film Commercial— Example One

Film Origination, HD Edit, and Delivery

This commercial's purpose is to entice millions of people to attend a particular movie. Super Bowl commercials have the unique challenge of having a huge audience, but because the air time is so expensive, it is usually only aired once during the program. There is a lot of pressure to make these commercials the best they can be. Although the approval process for Super Bowl commercials includes a lot more reviewing, most movie commercials go through the same basic process. In the past, it was only the Super Bowl commercials that were finished in high definition. Now, HD finishing is more common than not as more and more moviegoers are watching high definition broadcasts, both over the air and from cable or satellite providers.

The editing company that creates the commercial is called a trailer house, because the trailer is usually the beginning of a movie campaign. Most of the television commercials for movies use a portion of the original trailer. Actually, the entire run of commercials for a movie is usually based on the trailer. It is not uncommon for a trailer company to be exclusively dedicated to a motion picture production's advertising campaign.

The reason for this exclusivity is that feature film adverting is very demanding, and film executives like to work with people who are not only familiar with this type of campaign, but who also understand the amount of work necessary to make a product that satisfies so many people both at the studio and in the audience.

The producer and editor of the movie commercial are a team who work together to make the studio's vision a reality. Their main source of footage is the director's cut of the movie. A director's cut is the first assembly of the entire movie, which includes all the scenes that have been shot. Usually the director's cut is usually far too long to use as the final movie. So, the movie commercial is created from a source that is longer and contains more scenes than the one that will eventually be seen in the theater. However, since the best parts of the movie are often the ones used in commercials, it is rare that a shot used in the commercial is not actually in the movie.

Any Super Bowl commercial has a certain amount of prestige. It not only competes with other feature film commercials, it also competes with all the Super Bowl advertisements. As a side note, it is interesting that in 2006, the increase in high definition commercials was over 30%.

Because the feature film commercial is created almost entirely from existing film footage, very little original footage is used, if at all. The director's cut is output from the feature film company's editing system onto ¾-inch videotape, DVD, or DV tape, with a lot of text and numbers visually burned into the picture. These burn-ins pertain to the original feature film footage information, scene information, and audio time code information. Some burn-ins are used to trace

- The integration of commercials in a live high definition sporting event, not withstanding the Super Bowl, is interesting to watch in high definition. The groups of commercials, which some call "commercial islands," are often standard definition. These are easy to spot because standard definition commercials do not fill the high definition frame. More and more commercial islands have become at least partially filled with HD commercials. With closer examination, most of these commercials may have been shot, finished, and delivered in high definition, but they have been planned for simultaneous broadcast on both high definition and 4×3 NTSC. Graphics are placed in the center of the frame, or at least 4×3 safe, and the action is centered in the frame.
- It will take some time, but as more high definition sets and more programs are produced, directors and producers will be able to use the entire 16×9 frame for action and graphics.

back any pirated material and determine the source of the piracy. The entire feature film is captured into the trailer company's editing system at a low resolution. Since a trailer house usually works on several movies at any one time, they need to conserve space when capturing three-hour movies.

Using the film's trailer and the feature film footage, the commercial is edited in NTSC standard definition, usually in a 16 × 9 letterbox format. Because the original footage is transferred in NTSC and because most of the individuals who review the many versions of the commercial can only play or view NTSC, the entire creative process is done in NTSC standard definition.

Some studios have a direct optical fiber link from the editing room to executives' offices so that the executives can view the various cuts directly out of the nonlinear editing system into their office monitor. Hard copies that are output for cast or film staff approval are usually output to DVD, DV tape, or ¾-inch video. (In the past, VHS or ¾-inch Umatic tapes were used for approval.)

Feature film commercials always go through many versions and variations. Some are "killed" and never make it to the finishing process. This particular commercial made it through the gauntlet of approvals after version 11 was approved for high definition finishing.

It is worth mentioning that a commercial, whether for a movie or any other product or purpose, can be approved and totally finished, both visually and sound-wise, and still be "canceled" or "killed" before being broadcast. Just because a spot is finished does not mean it will be aired.

Anyway, once the feature film commercial is approved by all involved, there is a scramble to get all the needed high definition shots delivered to the finishing bay. This requires the actual film to be transferred to HD tape. In the early 2000s this was quite an ordeal, but by 2006 it had become common for studios to have a high definition copy of the feature film available. Of course, the HD copy of the extremely valuable unreleased feature film is always accompanied by a studio guard.

The final approved creative version is output from the nonlinear bay onto a ¾-inch NTSC videotape, DVD, or DV tape. In addition, an edit decision list (EDL) or Avid bin is emailed to the finishing bay

The delivery format requirements for this particular commercial to the studio were 1080psf23.98. This delivery, including textless copies along with all the audio tracks (narration, dialogue, effects, and both tracks of the stereo music), was to ensure that this commercial could be recreated in other formats. The reason for split audio tracks is to allow for this commercial to be "repurposed"; modified for other purposes like airline promos, broadcast sales, a shorter length, DVD commercials, or commercials in foreign languages.

The actual delivery format for the Super Bowl network was 720p59.94. This delivery was accomplished through a machine output down-conversion to the 720 frame size with a 3:2 pulldown introduced to create the conversion to 29.97 frames per second. The editorial process was performed on an "eQ," a Quantel online system that works on a priority software and hardware platform.

The ¾-inch reference tape is the "wrong" frame rate, but it is digitized and the resulting video clip is then sped up by 125%. This will be the visual reference that is used to conform the commercial. The EDL is printed as a hard paper reference, and then also converted in the eQ to get approximate high definition reference numbers both from the source material and where the edits fall on the timeline. (The eQ is also capable of accepting AAF files from Avid systems.)

The EDL was converted from 29.97 to the 23.98 frame rate required for delivery. The feature film is delivered, along with the required studio guard who ensures that the copy of the video is not duplicated. The required feature film material is digitized in high definition 1080i at 23.98 psf frames per second.

The company that edited the spot was not equipped to create graphics in high definition, so the graphics job was outsourced and they were created in 1080p23.98. These graphics were downloaded from an ftp site onto the same computer as the eQ editing system. The graphics were then imported into the editor and composited along with the already captured HD transfer of the original film footage. The credit block and accompanying legal information was hand typed using the titling tool in the eQ. And finally, the rating

Figure 6.5 The eQ editing system. Quantel's EQ is another HD editing system. This editing system utilizes proprietary software and hardware.

block was created by the finishing company's graphics department in high definition.

Most film commercials are created with versions: starts Friday, starts tomorrow, now playing, as well as textless and Canadian versions. This spot was no exception. Because this high definition commercial was to be viewed by most of the audience in a 4 × 3 standard definition format, titles and graphics had to stay within the 4 × 3 space. Although the commercial aired on the Super Bowl, other versions of the same commercial aired later in the month that followed.

A 1080psf23.98 D5 master was to be delivered to the studio with accompanying standard definition dubs.

Several issues were encountered during the completion of this spot. The first was that one shot was not in the feature and had to be telecined (transferred from 35-millimeter film to high definition video) in a separate telecine session. Also, the graphic was delivered in the wrong frame rate (59.94) and had to be redelivered in the correct rate of 23.98.

Conforming editor Chris Dingilian, who has had years of experience in conforming movie commercials in standard def and HD,
knows the pitfalls of taking an NTSC format as a video guide.
Feature film commercials are well known for their quick cutting
and occasional use of signal frames of white or other images for
quick transitions. "This is why we print out the EDL, "explained
Dingilian. "It is a manual process of examining the commercial for
potential short edits that are altered in speeding up of the NTSC
reference video." If there is a single-frame edit, it will show up in
the EDL. The time compression of the reference occasionally hides
one or two frame edits."

The commercial was finished and output to tape at the required
23.98 frame rate. This tape was put up on the optical fiber and
shown to the film executives in standard definition at a frame rate
of 29.97 with the playback deck introducing a 3:2 pulldown. With
some small alterations, the commercial was approved, and sent
dubbed to the network at 720p59.94.

Figure 6.6 Avid Symphony Editor Terrence Curran working at Alpha
Dog's Avid Symphony Editor. Alpha Dog is a post production company
located in Burbank, California. Avid is a major manufacturer of the
non-linear high definition editors with many different editor lines.

- Many creative editing systems either do not have the ability to convert a 29.97 sequence to a 23.98, or just are not willing to confront the issues involved with the frame rate conversions. Unlike the example of *That Guy* where the project was 23.98 frames per second from the beginning, trailer houses are not interested in revamping their entire offline infrastructure for one Super Bowl commercial a year.
- There are several problems with "eye matching" a 29.97 reference in a 23.98 project. First, the reference is sped up 125%, and in doing that, individual frames are often eliminated. Certainly this is not a huge problem; however, a single white flash, an often used transition in film commercials, can be lost in the speed up of the reference commercial. This is why the EDL is important. Since the commercial is short, a careful comparison and number count of the edits in the EDL and the ones created in the conform of the 23.98 high definition spot can identify the one or two frame edits that might not be seen in the frame conversion.

Frame rate conversion
29.95÷23.98 = 1.2497 (1.25)

Figure 6.7 *Let Me Count the Ways.* Another example of film and video professionals making film festival shots using high definition as an acquisition medium. (Photo provided by Vito J. Giambalvo.)

Let Me Count the Ways

HD Production, HD Post, HD Delivery

Let Me Count the Ways is a short dramatic film directed by Vito J. Giambalvo. Mr. Giambalvo started as a cameraman in popular sitcoms such as *All in the Family* and *Family Matters* and is now a director. The purpose of *Let Me Count the Ways* is to be a showcase for talent. It is intended to be entered into national and international film festivals.

With Mr. Giambalvo's years of production experience and no major effects work planned for the piece, the directorial challenge was very straightforward. There were no storyboards used in preparation for the shoot. As a matter of fact, the production was shot with a very low shooting ratio of 3 to 1.

The program was shot using a VariCam camera, one of the first series that Panasonic manufactured, because it was the only model available from the rental house at the time. The film was shot at 720p29.97 in a 4:2:2 color sampling rate on an HDCAM record deck. There was no "video village," and if there was a need to playback a take for any purpose, it was viewed through the camera's viewfinder.

DV dubs were created from the camera's original high definition masters. Included in the picture of the dubs was the time code of the original footage. Mr. Giambalvo took these DV tapes and captured them on his home computer and edited the entire program using iMovie, an Apple editing program.

Once the show was edited, a hand-written list of each edit was made. This list was then brought, along with the HDCAM camera originals, to Victory Studios. Here, using Final Cut Pro HD, the program was conformed. Using the hand-written list, all the cuts were assembled in the Final Cut program, using a DV output as a visual guide.

This program was then output from Final Cut onto a D5. The D5 was then brought to Technicolor, the well-known film and video company. The D5 was captured into an Avid Nitris DS, an online nonlinear editor. The purpose of this session was to color correct the program. The result of the color correction session was a new color corrected D5 at 720p29.97.

As a final step, the D5 was uprezed to HDCAM 1080i59.94 (1080i29.97). This format is used to make DVD and standard def NTSC copies to present to distributors and film festivals.

Super Bowl Feature Film Commercial— Example Two

Film Origination, HD Edit, and Delivery

This second commercial example was also originally created in a trailer house. The creative editing process took place in a 4 × 3 letterboxed project edited in standard definition NTSC (29.97). A ¾ visual reference video tape was delivered to the conforming facility, and was accompanied by an EDL in a computer file format.

The nonlinear finishing hardware and software used to deliver this high definition commercial was an Avid Symphony Nitris. This commercial was created for a different film studio than in the first example, yet the spot was heading to the same network for inclusion in the same Super Bowl program.

Although the commercial would be delivered in 720p59.94 to the ABC network, it was also finished in 1080psf23.98. The film studio had every intention of using this finished high definition commercial in other formats and frame rates.

The digitized reference copy was sped up by 125% as in the previous example, and an EDL was referenced for short edits. The EDL was converted from 29.97 to 23.98 using an Avid EDL converter. This is a software program that converts edit decision lists from one frame rate to another.

The feature film footage was digitized at full resolution at 1080psf23.98 at a 1:1 ratio; in other words, there was no compression used while capturing or editing. Since only an EDL was supplied for the finishing process, no effects came across to the online editing system. Ben Fortmiller, the online editor, recreated the effects in the spot. "It wasn't such a big deal," explained Fortmiller. "Previous spots from that trailer company had similar effects, so it wasn't like recreating something from scratch."

Graphics, including the rating block, credit block, and lower thirds, were supplied by a graphics company in 1080p23.98, downloaded, imported into the editor, and placed in the spot. Mr. Fortmiller made sure that the graphics remained in 4×3 safe title, so that even those watching the program in standard definition would be able to see the entire graphic.

- Although some creative editors do not like being "pigeonholed" as a certain type of editor, having prior experience in a particular situation or even working with a specific company can have its advantages. With over 18 years of exclusive experience conforming Walt Disney first-run theatrical commercials, I had prior knowledge of previous releases as well as the company's style of editing. Coming up with an online solution that fit the studio and the film's needs was much easier knowing the history of their movie campaigns.
- In addition, working with the same people and solving problems with them instilled a trust that helps in any situation when working with clients.

The commercial was onlined, checked, and then checked again. The spot was, like the previous example, output to tape at 1080psf23.98, and then played out over the optical fiber for the executives to approve in NTSC 29.97.

Once approvals were finalized, day and date versions were made, including a textless pass. The actual delivery of the commercial that played during the Super Bowl was a dub created by a conversion out of the high definition deck at 720p59.94 The result of this conversion was that there were six added frames through a 3:2 pulldown. Because this was a progressive output, the added frames were actually created as a "blend" by the HD deck. This process is similar, but visually different than the 2:3 pulldown that telecine machines create in film-to-tape transfers.

American Idol

This incredibly popular reality show is created in the editing bay. The producers, writer, and editors who can make an entertaining show out of hundreds of hours of footage are indeed talented. *American Idol* usually airs two different shows every week. Footage is shot in high definition at 720p59.94 using Panasonic high definition VariCam cameras. In the studio, Sony HDC-1500 cameras are used.

The creative editing process starts with capturing the incredible amount of footage at a 10:1 compression ratio. The footage is stored on a shared system (Avid Unity Media Network). With so much footage to be viewed and edited, there is obviously a large team that works on this show.

When a segment is approved, the sequence as an Avid File Exchange (AFE) computer file is sent on to an Avid DS Nitris. The *American Idol* program uses the Avid DNxHD 220 codec when redigitizing the HD material for the conforming session. The DNxHD 220 maintains the visual integrity of the HD signal, but compresses the data so that less space is taken on the computer's hard drives.

The short deadlines for the show require intense editing sessions. The multiple Avid systems can access footage at the same time, allowing freedom in postproduction choices.

However, the tightest turnaround times involve the live shows in which viewers see a recap at the end of the program, prompting them to call in their votes. Those recaps are actually shot at a rehearsal that ends at approximately 3:00 PM the same afternoon. This material must be edited, finished with titles, and delivered to the studio by 5:00 for live air to the East Coast.

Figure 6.8 *Tourgasm*: a high definition production for HBO. The HDV footage was transferred directly into a Symphony Nitris as uncompressed HD.

Dane Cook's *Tourgasm*

HDV Production, HD Post, HD Delivery

Tourgasm was one of HBO's first comedy documentary programs. The series follows the very funny and wildly popular comedian Dane Cook along with three other standup comedians, Gary Gulman, Robert "Bobby" Kelly, and Jay Davis, in a 30-day comedy tour across the United States. In this series, six of the eight programs were shot entirely in high definition on HDV at 1080i59.94. (Show eight was a combination of historical VHS footage and HDV. Show nine was a combination of HDCAM and HDV.)

The program was offlined using an Avid Adrenaline. The offline edit was performed in a standard definition NTSC project. Once the creative version of the show was approved, the sequence was posted at the company's internal computer network. Along with the sequence, a ¾ inch video tape was delivered to the finishing department as a visual reference and was conformed on a Symphony Nitris.

For offline, the HDV tapes were digitized using Avid's DNxHD compression codec at 10:1 in order to save computer drive space, as there were over 435 hours of footage used in the creation of the series.

Before the first show was approved, a test sequence of an early version of episode one was sent to the online bay. Several issues were discovered during the process of digitizing and comparing the offline reference copy and the online sequence (CCEC). Some of the offline time codes did not match the online taped because they had been dubbed. Also, the particular Miranda box had trouble locking up to the HDV tapes. These issues were quickly resolved by clean printing the questionable video sources. The Miranda issue was solved by manually digitizing the footage until a replacement Miranda was obtained.

The test and the show were digitized, with no compression from the HDV deck, into an Avid Symphony Nitris. The HDV deck was controlled by a Miranda, which acts as an in-between communications device between the HDV deck and the Symphony Nitris. As mentioned in an earlier chapter, the Miranda converts HDV signals into true HD.

The purpose of Miranda conversion was so that the online computer would not have to deal with HDV video.

Because of the many reels involved in the conform process, the small HDV deck as well as the Miranda conversion box were moved out of the central machine room, directly into the online bay. When a cut was sent out for final approval, the Avid bin for that show was posted on the company's server. The conforming editor then captured all the media that the cut would require. This procedure was called a "preload" where even though the final cut is not totally approved, the majority of the images in the preload will be used in the final delivery. Then, when the final approved show was posted, only the new, missing shots needed to be captured.

Dane Cook's *Tourgasm* involved hundreds of HDV tapes and thousands of individual shots. There were no video issues, not a single

Figure 6.9 *Tourgasm.* Shot almost entirely on HDV, this is an example of an HD show that moved through the postproduction process with few issues.

dropout or bad frame. The images were truly impressive, and with the DaVinci (a color correction system) artists Peter Swartz, Tom Martin, and Sam Dlugach, created a visually stunning show.

Once all the media had been captured, the show was checked for editorial accuracy against the ¾-inch offline, which had been digitized at 10:1 compression. Then the assembled program was output, textless, onto a high definition videotape at 1080i59.94.

The next step in the process was a color correction session. This was a comedy documentary shot in uncontrollable lighting situations; the colorists did an amazing job at leveling the various shots. The result of this color correction session was a textless videotape that was digitized back into the Symphony Nitris where text and credits were married to the color corrected program.

This final version of the program was output for delivery on HDCAM SR at 1080i59.94. Audio was laid back to the texted program, and then the entire show was sent to quality control. Once any quality control issues were addressed, the show was sent on to New York where HBO ran its own quality control check.

A textless version of the color corrected show was also delivered, with split tracks and a graphics pass that included the video fill as well as the alpha channel (also known as the matte, or holdout). This pass is used as an archival tape, as well as for international sales and for promotional uses. Both a texted and textless copy of the program was kept at the production house as a safety copy.

Tourgasm is a perfect example of how a high definition project with hundreds of hours of production footage can be edited and delivered in high definition. The HDV cameras and tape format were perfect for this type of "on the road documentary" comedy show.

Staring at the Sun

Film Production, HD Post, Film Delivery

Staring at the Sun is a presentation project shot on super 35 millimeter film. The camera negative was developed and then transferred to a high definition D5 video at 1080psf23.98. During the transfer, a rough color correction was applied to the film as it was transferred to D5. At the same time that the D5 image was being recorded, a simultaneous digital BetaCam was also being recorded. The image on the digital BetaCam had a series of information burned into the matte: the original film keycode, audio time code, the 23.98 time code from the D5, as well as the 29.97 frame time code.

This information was placed outside the picture area, in the matte line, for a purpose. The digital BetaCam footage in an offline editing system could be used for presentations by simply matting the burned-in information.

Staring at the Sun was a cuts only, dramatic program. The creative edit was accomplished using Apple's Final Cut Pro. The digital BetaCam footage was transferred to DVCam because the director/

Figure 6.10 Color correction bay. The art of color correction is often given to professionals with sophisticated equipment, specifically designed for this purpose. The textless program is recorded to tape, and then in a tape to tape process a new color corrected master is created. This media is loaded back into the nonlinear editor and texted.

editor did not want to rent a digital BetaCam and he had access to a DVCam.

The program was edited in standard 29.97 NTSC using non-drop frame time code. Once the program was finished, a DVCam reference was output as well as an old style CMX edit decision list (EDL).

The online conform was performed using an Inferno, a high-end editing and compositing system manufactured by Autodesk; this system is most often used to finish film trailers or film projects. The EDL was imported into the Inferno and converted back to a 23.98 EDL.

The D5 source material was captured into the Inferno. After a few small effects, several complex transitions, and titles created and added, the program was output in10-bit DPX files. These files were taken to FotoKem, a well-known film laboratory and video postproduction company in Burbank. The DPX files were color corrected and the entire 18-minute short was "recorded" or exposed to a film negative. This negative has since been used to make film prints of *Staring at the Sun*.

Kidney Thieves

Film Production, HD Post, HD Delivery

Kidney Thieves was shot and directed by the same director as *Staring at the Sun*. What director Toby Wilkins realized was that he rarely screened his 35 millimeter print of *Staring at the Sun*, and that a high definition master was more practical for a project than a film master. He had to rent a projector and a screening room just to view his 35 millimeter project.

The original production phase used super 16 film. The camera negative was developed and then transferred to HDCAM SR 4:4:4 (no color subsampling). This high quality color transfer allowed the maximum color recording possible for the upcoming color correction process. Again, during the transfer, a rough color correction was applied to the film as it was transferred to HDCAM SR video. And again, the simultaneous digital BetaCam contained the film keykode, audio time code, the 23.98 time code from the D5, as well as the 29.97 frame time code.

The creative editing was performed using Apple's Final Cut Pro. The program was edited in standard 29.97 NTSC. The online conform was performed in the Fire. The EDL was imported into the Inferno and converted to a 23.98 EDL.

The HDCAM source material was captured in the Inferno, conformed, and output again to HDCAM SR. In a tape-to-tape color correction session, the program was color corrected, then brought back into the Inferno. Once the color corrected program was captured in the Inferno, it was formatted. Titles were added and then the file was output to HDCAM SR 1080psf23.98. This master is capable of creating standard definition masters as well as introducing 2:3 pulldown to produce a 1080i59.94 program.

Unnamed HD DVD Project

HD Production, HD Post, HD Delivery

Due to legal reasons, the title of this project cannot be discussed; however, the online process did occur and the production can be seen on standard definition DVD and will also be seen when the movie's HD DVD is released.

This project was a high definition production intended as added content for the high definition DVD as well as a standard definition version of the same movie. It was shot with five cameras, including one that was mounted on a small movable crane. The production format was HDCAM, 1080psf23.98.

The show was offlined using an Avid nonlinear editor. The conforming of the program was performed on an Avid Nitris DS. The offline was edited in high definition 1080psf23.98. The original HD footage was compressed 3:1 and was captured using a DNxHD codec to save additional drive space. Once the program was approved, the offline sequence was posted on the company's internal server in an AAF (Advanced Authoring Format).

As a tribute to Avid's DNxHD, a group of experts could not tell the difference from the 3:1 DNxHD and the 1:1 uncompressed HD footage. Nevertheless, the show was redigitized and conformed at 1:1.

In the middle of the program is a short segment that was shot outside the studio location. The format used for the location shoot was 1080i59.94. This portion of the program was onlined at 1080i59.94, output to HD videotape at the same rate, and then played through a conversion device called Teranex. The result was a conversion from 1080i29.97 to 1080psf23.89. This tape was brought back to the Symphony Nitris, captured, and then inserted into the 1080psf23.98 sequence.

The end crawl encountered the same problems as *That Guy,* the first example described in this chapter. In order to eliminate the crawl's jitter, it either had to be sized in a very, very small font or be moving incredibly slowly. The decision was made to have the end credits in single card form.

The opening graphics and lower thirds were designed by The Studio at New Wave and were easily imported into the sequence. The delivery program output at 1080psf23.98 was chosen because the program was intended for future HD incorporation on HD DVD, but was included in the standard definition NTSC DVDs.

Kevin Smith

HD Production, HD Post, HD Delivery

Filmmaker Kevin Smith travels around the world speaking about his filmmaking experiences, and just about anything else that comes up during the events. At two of these cities, his fascinating talks were captured on high definition. These lectures were shot with multiple cameras with the express purpose of being offered on DVD in high definition and standard definition. Shot at 1080 psf23.98, this over four-hour show is another example of a high definition program that can sail smoothly through an HD process.

The creative editing utilized the Avid DNxHD codec again to save computer drive space, as the two separate programs totaled over four hours. With five cameras, there was a lot of media to choose from.

The creative process took place in an Avid nonlinear editor and was cut using a combination of traditional editing and the multicam option at 23.98. Once the two lectures and the five added content programs were approved, the conforming process began.

Because the editors did not want to deliver compressed media, the two lectures and five added content programs were redigitized at a full 1:1 ratio with no compression. Color correction was performed in the Symphony Nitris and the final product was output to D5.

The 5.1 Dolby surround mix was laid back to the D5 and delivered for high definition and standard definition DVDs.

A Place to Rest My Head

HDV Production, HDV Post, HD Delivery

After a year of writing the script and four weeks of preproduction preparation, director Kris Brown and his international crew shot for six days in and around La Cañada, California. Shot on a JVC GY-HD100U at 720p23.98, the six hours of HDV footage was digitized using a JVC BR-HD50U Pro-HD Recorder/Player into Adobe Premiere Pro 2 using the downloaded JVC plug-in specifically for the JVC ProHd codec.

Audio was recorded on a Fostex digital audio recorder. However, there was no time code sent to the audio recorder during production. While editing, Kris Brown manually related the time from the scene's head slate to the start of the clips used to audio designer Elliot Hartley. In addition, a low resolution QuickTime file was used for a visual reference in order to mix audio to picture. Hartley used the various audio sources with his own original music and effects to create a mix using Protools on his Apple G4 computer.

Figure 6.11 A night shot being prepared for one of the 20 scenes in the project called *A Place to Rest My Head*. Shot over six days, the project had a shooting ratio of 16:1. (Photo by Ben Taylor.)

The final audio mix was output as a WAVE file and delivered to Brown who imported it and married it with the final cut of the HDV footage. Editing went smoothly using the somewhat under-powered desktop computer (a 3-gigahertz Pentium 4 processor with a 1-gigabyte memory), but the JVC plug-in did not support videotape output. As a result, the textless edited program, along with its accompanying mix, was output in a series of uncompressed QuickTime files from Premiere at 1080p23.98. These files were then imported into an Avid Symphony Nitris. The files were combined into the Nitris timeline and then output to a Panasonic D5.

The D5 was then brought to Modern VideoFilm in Burbank where, a tape-to-tape session was performed using a DaVinci color correc-tion device. The color timed master was then reimported into an Avid Symphony Nitris. In the Symphony, front and end titles were added to the project. The final program was to a D5 at 1080psf23.98, which can be used to output to many different formats.

Figure 6.12 The crew of *A Place to Rest My Head* sets up for a car accident shot at night. This project, although only costing $8,000, had over $50,000 worth of donated equipment and services. Shot on HDV at 720p23.98, the master resides on a D5 at 1080p23.98. (Photo by Ben Taylor.)

Top Secret Project

HD Production, HD Post, HD Delivery

This project is destined to be broadcast on a high definition cable station, but the project will not be finished before mid 2007; the workflow has recently been established. The project is to be delivered in 1080i59.94; however, much of the footage has already been shot at 720p59.94 using a Panasonic AG-HVX200, DVCPRO HD camera. Since there are no proxy files with this media and since it is going to be onlined and offlined using Avid editing systems, a workflow has been established to accommodate the other frame rates that will be included in the footage (1080p29.97 and 1080i59.94).

For the offline/creative process, the P2 media is edited at full resolution in a 720p59.94 project. The other tape-based footage will be down converted to 720p59.94 and captured at 20:1 to save on drive space. Once the project is edited and approved, it is sent to the online bay as a 720p59.94 project.

The P2 media will quickly relink. The tape-based materials will be captured at full 1:1 resolution down converted from the HD deck. The conformed project will be output to a 720p59.94 tape, and then brought back into the Avid at 1080i59.94 for texting and color correction.

Every Network Has Its Own Rules

Take a look at any cable offering and you quickly can tell there are many, many networks that purchase and produce video programming. Some of the channels are owned by the same parent company. Yet the delivery requirements of even related companies can vary.

Networks' delivery standards vary because of technical requirements, programming necessities, and other internal issues. From placement of bars and tone, to how the textless version of the program is to be delivered, each company expects a delivered program to meet specific standards. It is a necessity to keep in constant communication with any client about their high definition needs, as there are far too many choices to leave anything to chance.

CHAPTER 7

Other Editing Issues

Viewing HD

Now that you are planning to shoot and edit a high definition show, what kind of monitor do you need? There are several types of monitors that can display a high definition signal: tube (also known as CRT which stands for Cathode Ray Tube), DLP (Digital Light Processing), plasma, and LCD (Liquid Crystal Display). For most professional uses, a calibrated tube monitor is considered the most accurate. However, CRTs are quickly becoming a technology of the past. Broadcasters still use CRTs in edit bays and machine rooms to view high definition signals; however, the days of the CRT are numbered. Inherently interlaced, heavy, needing constant calibration, and unable to accurately display high frequencies, CRTs are soon to be replaced. DLPs, Plasma and LCDs are being used in tech bays and monitoring stations in greater numbers.

Brightside Technologies has a $50,000 LCD monitor designed for true color reference. And in early 2006, NEC (Nippon Electronics Corporation) announced an adjustable LCD, which is not lit from behind with standard diffused florescent light, but instead uses two strips of arrayed red, green, and blue LEDs. This monitor is more affordable at about $7,000. eCinema has said it would be introducing its 40-inch LCD by the fourth quarter of 2006, and that its improvement in the LCD would bring it to the level of CRT quality.

Some edit bays use consumer flat screens, but in many cases these may not be the best choice for color approval. The inability of many of these displays to be critically adjusted limits their usefulness.

Figure 7.1 Brightside Technologies. Brightside Technologies has developed methods of increasing the contrast range in LCD monitors. Using this technology, the usual "gray" blacks are eliminated. (Photo courtesy of Brightside Technologies).

However, there are converters that address the interlacing issues and pixel-to-pixel comparison needed for quality control and color correction finesse. One such device is BMD's (Blackmagic Design) HDlink, which converts HD into a high quality signal that can be viewed on computer display screens.

Likewise, consumer electronic devices are improving by the month. Where LCDs and plasma televisions were once playthings of the rich, they have dropped in price and increased dramatically in quality. Plasma, LCD, and DLP all operate differently and have their strengths and weaknesses.

From a consumer point of view, all of these displays work well and produce acceptable pictures. The current strengths and weakness

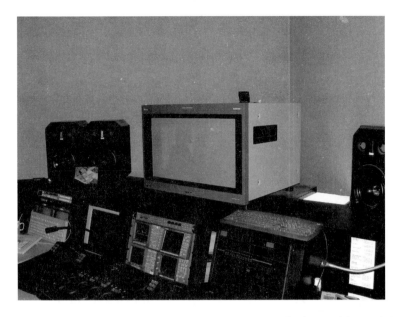

Figure 7.2 CRT monitor. The heavy, interlaced, and often calibrated CRT monitor is slowly being replaced by flat screen monitors.

of each type are listed below. But remember that it only takes three months for a new model or upgrade to alter the limitations of any of these displays. It is unwise to purchase that less expensive "off brand" screen as cheaper monitors tend to have more of the inherent flaws of that particular type.

LCD Monitors

The LCD display is created through the use of three liquid crystal cells. In front of these cells is a red, green, or blue filter. Light, which is shone from behind, passes through these filtered cells. The filter is responsible for creating the colors on the screen. The back light is why it has a little more trouble reaching dark blacks.

Strengths and weaknesses:

Higher native resolution
Consume less power

Lighter weight

Less prone to burn-in

Tendency to display "gray for black" colors

Inherent delay on fast-moving images although mostly noticeable on larger (36 + screens); this issue can be more relevant for lower refresh rate screens

Brighter in daylight conditions

Better appearance of black in bright conditions

Plasma Screens

Plasma displays use a matrix of tiny gas plasma cells to create an image.

Strengths and weaknesses:

Larger screens

Heavier

Display black images better (unless room is brightly lit)

Brighter color

Wider angle of display

Cheaper, especially in the larger screen sizes

Prone to burn-in, false contouring artifacts, and posterization of shadows

DLP Monitors

DLP uses a proprietary chip invented by Texas Instruments. On the surface of the chip are thousands of tiny mirrors representing pixels. As light is shone onto these mirrors, they change in angle. If the mirror is one way, it reflects light on the screen (on), if it is facing the other way (off), it reflects the light away from the screen. These mirrors are capable of switching on and off thousands of times per second.

Strengths and weaknesses:

Shorter bulb life

12" or more wide

Superb for large screen projection

Used in electronic cinema projection

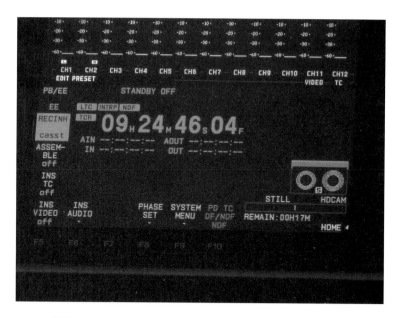

Figure 7.3 HDCAM SR time code. Just to the right of the "System Menu" is the time code display on an HDCAM SR. Converting 23.98 to 29.97, the deck can play out either drop or non-drop time code. This can cause problems if the wrong setting is selected.

Time Code Display from High Definition Decks

The high definition playback deck is an amazing machine. It not only plays myriad high definition images at different frame rates, it can also introduce 3:2 pulldown, output standard definition signals, change time code output from drop to non-drop, or change 23.98 time code to 29.97. There is a menu with hundreds of options, depending on which frame rate is being played back.

Considering all the options and possibilities, it is easy to have an erroneous setting on a high definition deck. For example, digitizing a 23.98 tape with a different time code output than was originally digitized will cause a "time code break" as minutes are crossed. It is a good idea to check all parameters when digitizing media, or when constant aborts happen. It could be a simple matter of switching a play out or time code menu. Also, when playing out a 23.98 tape at 29.97, you have the choice of displaying drop or non-drop time code.

Understanding Different Aspect Ratios in SD

Standard definition images will continue to be used in high definition programming. It is helpful to understand these issues as long as the integration of standard definition and high definition continues.

Letterboxed ratios in the 4 × 3 standard definition space were originally a result of a film-to-tape telecine of a film production. In the early days of letterboxing feature transfers, at-home audiences were annoyed at the black margins they saw at the top and bottom of the screen. As letterboxed images became accepted by television viewers, more and more films were transferred to widescreen and video programs began to be shot in the 16 × 9 format.

It is interesting to note that many films are shot on a 35 millimeter film frame, which is itself a 4 × 3 image. During the postproduction process, the image is cropped at the top and bottom to create the illusion of a widescreen image. The common film aspect ratios are 1:66, 1:77 (actually 16 × 9), 1:85, and 2:35.

A normal 4 × 3 image is expressed as a ratio of 1:33. This was the original ratio that film was shot in before television became a competitor for viewers' attention. Film producers decided to make widescreen movies in order to differentiate the theater experience from that of watching television.

The aspect ratio of high definition is 16 × 9 or 1:77. So, if one intends to fill the entire screen with a standard definition image, image ratios of 1:85 and 2:35 will lose images at the sides as they will have to be blown up past the vertical edges of the high definition frame. 1:77 fits nicely. However, filling the high definition frame with a standard definition 4 × 3 ratio image will end up with a portion of the image being lost at the top and bottom of the frame. This assumes that the 4 × 3 image will be enlarged from the center. Adjustments should be made during editing to choose which part of the image will be lost.

It is worth mentioning that "blowing up" a standard definition frame to fit a high definition frame will degrade the image quality as it will have to be enlarged by over 300%.

The 1:85 aspect ratio is very close to 1:77. If a 1:85 film is transferred to high definition, the result will be a very small black matte at the top and bottom of the high definition frame. It is hard to see, but several of the 2006 Super Bowl commercials were made from 1:85 feature transfers. This format does not entirely fill the screen unless blown up about 4%. The 2:35 image will have quite a large matte at the top and bottom of the HD frame.

As mentioned earlier, the UK's BBC network uses a 14:9 process, which is a compromise between losing the sides of a 16×9 image with a full frame 4×3, and a full letterbox showing a 16×9 image on a 4×3 screen. A 16×9 program is shot with the essential action in the 14:9 portion of the frame. The program is electronically tagged for a 14×9 display.

When inserting a 4×3 standard definition image into a 16×9 high definition, the 4×3 image can be treated several different ways. It can be placed on an HD background, preserving the 4×3 ratio. It can also be blown up to reach the sides of the 16×9 frame, but as a result the top and bottom of that frame will be cut off. Often, vertical adjustments must be made to choose the best portion of the 4×3 frame to be displayed in the 16×9 space. Or the 4×3 can be placed so that the top and bottom of the frame reach the top and bottom of the 16×9 frame. This results in black margins (often called pillar boxes) where the image does not reach the horizontal edges.

Edit System Compatibility

Completing a visual production is complicated no matter what the length of the project. There is no reason to make the process any harder. As discussed earlier, the translation of effects from one edit system to another is difficult at best. Unless a program is based on cuts, one should always offline and online using compatible software.

Cross-platform compatibility from offline systems to a different brand of finishing computer can work. One of the cross-platform tricks is to use AVX effects, third party computer programs (Boris,

Sapphire, 3Prong, Artel, etc.), that can be installed in different brands of nonlinear editing systems. These effects can also be used in online systems. This is one way to ensure the effects created and approved in the creative part of postproduction can be matched during the conforming process. You will need to make sure that the plug-in works on both the offline and online systems (CCEC). Testing the compatibility of an edit list that includes planned effects is highly recommended.

Despite the potential of getting effects to move across platforms, one should always online using the same compatible platform that the program was offlined on. Cross-platform editing is usually not worth the effort or cost, unless the program is based on cuts and all effects are being done from cut to cut, not dependent on the editing program to create those effects. (Effects would be created elsewhere and the final version added to the final edited program.)

There are also computerized programs (like Automatic Duck) specially designed to "translate" edit sequences from one brand of editing system to another. Again, tests of the compatibility between different edit systems should be made long before a delivery deadline is close.

Ideally, the high definition workflow should not include experimenting unless there is plenty of lead time. The path taken should be known, well traveled, and create as few problems as possible. After all, selling, planning, shooting, and editing a high definition visual program is hard enough. There should not be additional challenges due to technology mismatches or incompatibility.

Most professionals do not attempt to cross computer programs or even operating platforms between offline and online unless absolutely necessary. If crossing platforms becomes a necessity, one should make several tests to ensure that any questionable effects will be read and performed accurately in the online system.

There are computer file formats specifically designed to move editorial information from one system to another. The oldest and simplest of these formats is the EDL (Edit Decision List). The EDL was designed for linear editing and provides limited effects information. For a film, or a simple cuts-only program, this format of exchange could work at a basic level.

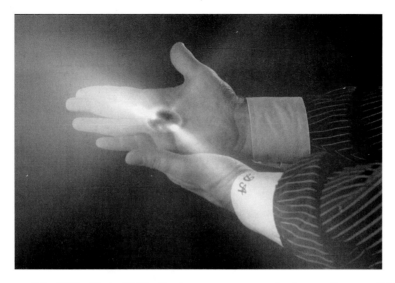

Figure 7.4 AVX effect. AVX effects are very popular in nonlinear editing systems. These are third party effects that can be used in offline and online situations.

Further up the scale in program translation are AAF (Advanced Authoring Format), ALE, (Avid Log Exchange), and the proposed MXF (Material Exchange Format) files. Quantel supports the AAF format. Why? Because there are so many Avid offline systems in use and Quantel sells many finishing machines.

Final Cut Pro has an export tool. Its files have an "XML" extension. Adobe's Premiere Pro and Leitch's Velocity also support and export AAF files, but again, any AVX, proprietary effects, or other plug-in effect should definitely be tested before compatibility with a finishing system is assumed.

The Preload

One workflow process that has proven effective is called the "preload." Since it can take a long time to load footage for an online conform, it has proven effective to load the media for a project that is in the very final stages of approval. For instance, a producer/editor team may have reached the point where a deadline is days away and the cut is finished and being sent to the client for the final time. Reasonably sure that there will be few, if any changes, the program could be sent to the conforming online bay and the media could be loaded. This of course makes the assumption that the online editing system has the digital storage to hold this media until the final approval comes. However, when the final sequence arrives, only the new footage is loaded.

Testing Workflow and Media Accuracy

If there is time, it's always a good idea to get a sequence even if the program has not been finished or approved just to test the accuracy of tapes, time code, and effects translation to the online system. It is better to identify problems before they affect delivery schedules. Often there are simple fixes that can be made early in the editorial process rather than suddenly being surprised with a problem that could have been avoided.

Edit System Updates

The speed at which high definition software is being updated and improved is incredible. Editing, compositing, DVD burning, and other high definition programs continue to improve and evolve. These programs are constantly adding new formats and codecs. Keeping programs up to date not only makes editing easier, the need for workarounds and tricks is often eliminated as programmers find direct ways to accomplish common tasks. Also, as new equipment is brought to the marketplace, it only takes months for editing programs to accommodate the new hardware. Sometimes it is just a simple matter of going to the company's Web site and downloading updates.

Intermediate Codecs Versus "Native" Editing

Intermediate codecs convert an original video format into a different one for editing purposes. These codecs are used in editing and then one can output the project from that codec to the delivery format.

In some systems, when an effect is created, the codec is returned to the original video format, and the effect created is then encoded again. This constant processing can degrade the original video.

Editing natively involves the ability to capture footage in its original codec (HDV, DVCPRO HD, XDCAM, etc.) and edit using that codec. The output can be put back to tape or file using that codec, or the program can be converted to other formats (HD, MPEG2, etc.).

Data Management

A frame of video takes up a finite amount of space on a computer's hard drive. How that frame was recorded and captured determines how much space that frame occupies. Computers do not work well when their hard drives are full. As mentioned earlier, most experts suggest that one should not work with drives that are over 80% full. A full computer drive slows performance and increases the risk of a drive failure.

Many editors store copies of the edit file on backup media. The small USB memory sticks are perfect for this type of file protection. Another quick way to protect valuable files from loss is to email them to yourself and store them in your Internet service provider's mailbox.

It is a necessity to have ample hard drive space for your creative and finishing needs. There are calculators within editing machines and a few can be found online. One is at http://www.rorke.com/avcalc/index.cfm and another is at http://www.digital-heaven.co.uk/Videospace widget

In order to do this calculation correctly, you will have to know the frame size of your project. There are tricky aspects to this, because all 1080 or 720 projects are not the same. There are codecs that can reduce the file size of an HD frame.

Data Protection

Most nonlinear editing systems have an option to save data at regular intervals. One of the first actions in setting up an edit program should be to make sure that the "autosave" function is enabled and set to a reasonable time. In larger projects, it can be ineffective to save often, as this process takes up valuable work time. However, it is a good idea to completely save a project at the end of a shift, not on the drives with your stored media, but either on the system drive or on a removable drive.

Mixing Frame Rates

As mentioned earlier, mixing frame rates is not advisable, but there are situations where it is unavoidable. The issue of frame size can be troublesome also. A 1080 image placed next to a standard definition (720 × 480) image totally reveals the lack of resolution of the smaller image. The standard definition image, blown up to fill the frame, will always look somewhat soft. A 720-sized frame is not a reach for a 1080 program. Some experts think a 720 progressive frame will end up equal to a 1080i frame because it is progressive; however, the same interlacing process will be applied to that progressive frame when broadcast, and will thus reduce the image quality.

There are editing systems that are more forgiving than others when it comes to frame rates. Others refuse to even import alternative frame rates. Again, talking with the post facility, checking the current downloads, and communicating with everyone involved can head off problems before they become nightmares (CCEC).

Fixing It Yourself

Some nonlinear editors do have frame rate converters in their software. For instance, Apple has a utility called Compressor that is included in their Final Cut Pro Studio. This program will alter a scene, movie, or sound file. It will convert NTSC to PAL, PAL to NTSC, SD to HD, and so forth. However, if you do not have this option, the actual speed of the clip will have to be changed and the conversion may result in motion artifacts. One of the tools to disguise this artifact is an effect called a motion blur. Used sparingly, this effect can smooth out jerky shots. If your editor does not have this program, it can be obtained from effects companies such as Vision Effects' ReelSmart Motion Blur (www.revisionfx.com/mblur. htm). Again, any type of effect that blurs the image will result in a lessening of resolution.

Credit Rolls in the 23.98 Frame Rate

The 23.98 frame rate can cause issues in rolls. A roll is the vertical movement of a credit sequence. If the font size is large or the roll moves too fast, the text appears to jitter as it moves. In many cases, single cards cut together provide a much better solution. In order to eliminate the jitter in a roll, the font has to be extremely small, move slowly, or both.

This issue is not as troublesome in film because the small characters used in the end credits are blown up across a large movie screen, essentially making small words huge. In high definition, however, most individuals are viewing on much smaller screens. Thus, if the characters are kept at the size one views them in the theater, the words on the credit roll, when viewed on a HD screen, are usually too small.

- In my experience, rolls in a frame rate of 23.98 are troublesome. There is an inherent flicker if the roll moves too fast or the text is too large. I would suggest single cards at this frame rate because the type size can be larger and read easier.
- However, if there is a need to make a roll, the following is a suggestion from an experienced coworker regarding how to deal with crawls at 23.98:
- A good rule of thumb is rates that are *even* multiples of the field rate and to stay away from *odd* multiples of the field rate. So, for 23.976 you might want to try 96, 192, 288, 384, and 480 [pixels per second].

Organization and Data Protection

The process of creating, shooting, editing, and finishing a visual project is always challenging. One of the most important chores during a production is to keep track of the many sources, contacts, reels, audio CDs, and numerous other pieces of information. Scripts, production notes, editing suggestions, and delivery requirements need to be duplicated and filed. It is very disheartening to spend half a day looking for a scene or reel that has been carefully vaulted, but no one knows where.

Another form of protection is to make sure sequences are labeled with dates. This makes it easier to find auto protection files of edit sequences. In terms of nonlinear editing, most systems have the ability to create bins. Because there are so many types of data that are stored in these systems, bins for specific purposes should probably be created. Depending on the type of project, bins could be organized in scenes with additional ones for effects, color correction, and titling.

Time Management

It takes time to shoot a program, even with detailed planning. It takes a long time to edit a show. Allowing sufficient time to accomplish all the chores of a production and its associated postproduction process is crucial to its success. One aspect that is commonly overlooked is the conforming of a project. The online process that takes place after the creative editing entails not only the finishing aspect, but also quality control and duplication of the program. It is rare that a finished project will go through a quality control check without some issue arising. It takes time to address these problems too.

Politics

Throughout the creation of a visual program, dealing with people can be as important as dealing with equipment. Any show has a hierarchy of authority, and being able to deal with all levels of authority is almost a necessity. Being kind, patient, and willing to listen can be as valuable as being a skilled craftsman.

The Newest Fad

Sometimes products are brought to the marketplace before they are really ready for use. Companies that do this type of thing depend on their customers to find the less obvious flaws in their product. The hope is that in subsequent versions, these "bugs" will be corrected.

Unless there is some pressing reason to use a new product, it would be a good idea to let someone else do the experimental work. Putting together a visual production is hard enough. There is no reason to make it any more difficult.

Connections

There is no end to the number of people in the video and film world who would like nothing more than to help out. Of course, not everyone can dedicate his or her entire life to working. But many professional actors, directors, editors, and writers will donate their time, or certainly charge less than their going rate in order to be involved with a promising production. Keeping a file of people you meet on your journey is vital when it comes time to pool your resources.

Keeping It Simple

Mixing frame rates, using different offline and online systems, mixing cameras or brands of tape stock—there are so many way to make a complex situation even more convoluted. High definition production can be a painless and relatively simple process. Knowing the production's delivery frame, keeping that rate a constant throughout the post-process, and constantly communicating with everyone can make a high definition experience a positive one.

Chapter Seven Summary

- CRTs are quickly being eliminated because of the intense interest in flat screen (LCD and plasma) displays.

- Consumer electronics devices are improving by the month. Although LCDs and plasma televisions were once playthings of the rich, they have dropped in price and increased dramatically in quality.

- Plasma, LCD, and DLP all operate differently and have various strengths and weaknesses.

- It only takes a few months for a new model or upgrade to come along and alter the limitations of any of these display types.

- There are many menu options on high definition video machines. It is a good idea to check all parameters when digitizing media, or when constant aborts happen.

- Many films are shot on a 35 millimeter film frame, which is itself a 4 × 3 image.

- The common film aspect ratios are 1:66, 1:77, 1:85, and 2:35.

- The aspect ratio of high definition is 16 × 9, or 1:77.

- When a 1:85 film is transferred to high definition, the result will include a very small black matte at the top and bottom of the high definition frame.

- The 2:35 image will have quite a large matte at the top and bottom of the 16 × 9 frame.

- A 4 × 3 frame blown up to fill the sides of the 16 × 9 frame will result in some loss of the image, either at the top or the bottom or both, depending on how the frame is vertically positioned.

- If the 4 × 3 image placed in the 16 × 9 frame reaches just to the top of the frame, the result will be black margins at the sides of the frame. These black margins are often called pillar boxes.

- Testing of the compatibility of cross-platform editing is a necessity long before an online edit begins.

- There are computerized programs (like Automatic Duck) specially designed to "translate" edit sequences from one brand of editing system to another.

- Many professionals do not attempt to cross computer programs or even operating platforms between offline and online unless absolutely necessary.

- If crossing platforms becomes a necessity, one should make several tests to ensure that any questionable effects will be read and performed accurately in the online system.

- Generally speaking, a cuts-only project is easy to move from one program to another. Even the decades-old Edit Decision List format will suffice for online applications. However, if there are effects, especially those that are specific to that particular program, there can be compatibility issues.

- There are computer file formats specifically designed to move editorial information from one system to another: the EDL (Edit Decision List), AAF (Advanced Authoring Format), ALE (Avid Log Exchange), and the proposed MXF (Material Exchange Format) file formats.

- Final Cut Pro has an export tool called "XML."

- Keeping programs current is a necessity. It is usually a matter of going to the software company's Web site and downloading updates.

- Editing natively involves the ability to capture footage in its original codec (HDV, DVCPRO HD, XDCAM, etc.) and edit using that codec. The output can be recorded back to tape or file using that codec, or the program can be converted to other formats (HD, MPEG2, etc.).

- Computer drives should not be filled to more than 80% of capacity, because over-filled drives will slow performance and increase the risk of a drive failure.

- The small USB memory sticks are perfect for storing editorial sequences and other vital information.

- It is a good idea to save a project regularly and at the end of a shift, not on the drives with your stored media, but either on the system drive or on a removable drive.

- In many cases, single cards cut together provide a much better solution than credit rolls in 23.98 projects.

- Being able to deal with all levels of authority is a great skill to have.

- Unless there is some pressing reason to use a new product, it would be a good idea to let someone else experiment with new equipment and work out the kinks.

- Keeping a file of people one meets on the journey is vital when it comes time to pool one's resources.

- Keep it simple, always.

CHAPTER 8

HD, Film, and Digital Intermediates

High definition has been used as a production medium for more than a few major feature films and its use is growing rapidly. The digital intermediate (DI) process, once used only for high profile, high budget films, has been used by all levels of productions from HD film presentations to medium budget features to Hollywood summer blockbusters.

Two *Star Wars* movies were shot on high definition; however, most of the images in those films were created in a computer. The high resolution backgrounds of the Star Wars world are created as CGIs (computer generated images). These images are then married with the green screen footage that was shot on high definition. The stylized film *Sin City*, the Western *Once Upon a Time in Mexico*, the effects-laden *Spy Kids*, as well as *Shark Boy and Lava Girl*, are all products of Robert Rodriguez's Texas-based production company and were shot in high definition video. There are also cameras like the Thompson/Grass Valley Viper FilmStream™ that output data, rather than actual video. As another example of the power of the DI process, not only to integrate multiple frame sizes, James Cameron used HD *and* DV footage in his IMAX presentation of *Ghosts of the Abyss*.

The first DI processes were very expensive. Computer storage for the large data files, software to manipulate those files, and the equipment to expose film to the finished files were new and very costly. Now, with storage and computing costs dropping, many film postproduction companies have invested in the large data infrastructure required for the DI workflow. In a few short years, the DI business, once an exclusive process reserved for expensive effect shots, has been embraced by the entire film community.

The great advantage of the DI process is that it can be designed as a very high-end, expensive workflow, or conversely, much of the work can be done in high definition using desktop power and home computer drives without including the expensive portions until the very end.

It is not uncommon for low budget films to shoot HD video and edit in a high definition environment before entering the DI suite. Some producers of low budget film–destined projects will conform their movie in a non-linear editor, then output to HD videotape and bring that tape to the DI suite for color correction, effects, and titles, and finally output to film. This workflow can be done using a relatively inexpensive computer setup, and can be very cost effective when working through the high definition DI process.

Some filmmakers who prepare their project in a high definition workspace, either at a facility, or in a desktop environment, used the creative editing software to create DV or DVD copies of the production to secure additional funds.

Once more money has been located, the high definition video master can be used as a source to create computer files in the DI suite, which are then run through the digital intermediate process. The final result is an output to film for projection in theaters.

Others choose to begin the DI process, loading files and starting color correction, but then output portions of it to show potential investors. When additional monies are acquired, the DI process can continue at full speed.

Because more often than not, producers in search of additional funds output their projects in NTSC standard definition media, the original production footage is often shot at 23.98 rather than true 24 frames per second. With 23.98, slowing of the footage is not necessary to match the 29.97 NTSC frame rate.

Not only does the DI offer multiple, pristine film negatives for creating theatrical prints, it also ensures a "true to the original" high

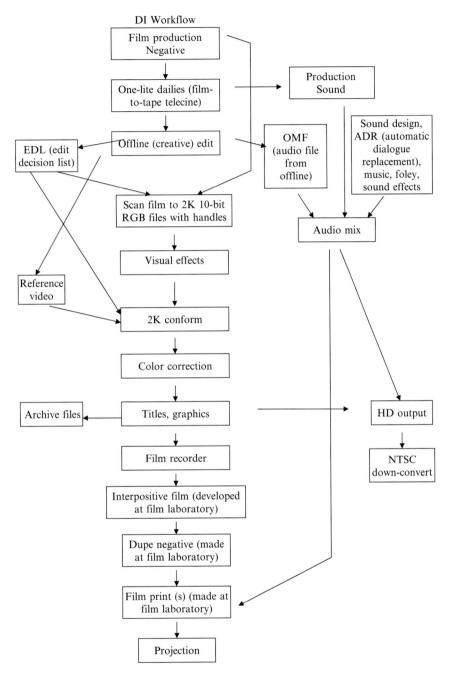

Figure 8.1 DI Workflow

definition as well as standard definition master for ancillary markets (like "pay-per-view," airline sales, and DVDs). Formerly, the camera negative-to-projection print process resulted in multiple generations of film, which in turn reduced the resolution of the final film print. The DI process avoids much of the film generation degradation, maintaining much of the original negative's quality. Ultimately, the Digital Intermediate process has become a much sought-after and highly regarded technology.

From small independent movies to large-budget ones like *Miami Vice, Rent, Collateral,* and *King Kong,* DI has revolutionized the film postproduction process.

HD for Feature Film

With frame rates of 23.98 and 24 frames per second, high definition is a natural fit for filmmakers. The current trend is to record log files or raw files stored directly onto hard drives, or in some cases, dual video recorders. Raw video files are files of data taken directly from a camera without any processing to turn them into readable or standard files. In the DI suite, there are programs that can take this raw data and convert them into pictures. The purpose of recording the raw files is to store as much of the original data from the camera as possible.

It is interesting to note, however, that the confusion over frame rates persists. Both 23.98 and 24 are used by filmmakers as viable frame rates. Many filmmakers specifically choose 23.98 because this frame rate is easily compatible with NTSC and 1080i59.94, and especially if their project is heading to HDTV or even standard definition NTSC. Also, as mentioned earlier, 23.98 is an easy output to SD and is often used to solicit additional finishing funds. Many filmmakers swear by a true 24 frames per second frame rate.

It is very important to contact the company you intend to use for your DI work. The actual technical aspects of the HD frame rates, color sampling, and even tape format should be discussed well ahead of any production. Feature film producers almost always budget for tests to examine new cameras, lighting, and other aspects, to ensure the money that is spent on real production is not wasted. It is much easier to work out technical details before the talent and other crew members create much more expensive costs just for shooting tests.

The Details

Generally speaking, there are three standard sizes of images that the digital intermediate workflow encompasses: high def, 2k, and 4k.

The 2k and 4k are computer files that are created as a film telecine machine scans the image on the film and translates that frame into data. A 4k file is huge and few productions, at this point in time, can afford the cost associated with thousands of files that size to flow through the DI process. There are professionals who predict that HD 2k and 4k cameras will be introduced in early 2007.

When one uses high definition as a production medium, the show is offlined using down-conversions of the footage. Once the program is edited, the HD images to finish are scanned into the DI computer. The scanner can be a telecine capable of converting the film image into data or an actual film scanner.

Shoot HD, Edit Offline, Conform HD, Enter DI, Output Film

The HD to film workflow has several possible paths. One is where the show is creatively edited on a nonlinear editing system; the footage necessary to finish the film is scanned using a telecine, and the nonlinear editing system provides an EDL. Now, the necessary high definition material is scanned into the DI system. The result is a series of computer files stored on a hard drive. Color correction and effects work can be accomplished at this point. For complicated effects work, the DI files are sent to an effects facility. These effects can be created within the same company that is performing the DI work, or at a completely different company.

Shoot Film, Edit Offline, Cut Film Negative, Enter DI, Output Film

Another way to utilize DI is to transfer the film to video dailies, creatively edit, obtain a cut list from the nonlinear editor, cut the film negative, and then only scan the assembled reels of film negative.

This process of scanning a film also allows for choices as to how big the file is. A full-aperture "4K" scan has 4096 pixels horizontally, and 3112 pixels vertically. 4K is a very expensive process, but its purpose is to capture the most image information to allow the highest quality of digital manipulation. 2K scans are less expensive and more common: 2048 × 1556 pixels to each frame. They yield files that are only a quarter the size of 4K scans: about 13 MB vs. 52 MB per frame. In comparison, a 16 × 9 high definition frame has 1920 pixels vertically.

The pixel counts from film frames are taken from a 4 × 3 image, an image that will be cropped on the top and bottom. The size of the file has a direct relationship to the cost of the digital intermediate process. However, costs associated with drives that store these frames continue to drop. Competition among film postproduction companies is also a factor in the dropping costs of the DI process.

Once the film is scanned, either in 2K or 4K files, the film is conformed to the creative edit. Effects, color correction, and titles are added. But the DI process offers additional benefits as well. Changes are much faster in the DI suite than in the traditional film processes. Multiple versions for previews can be output and it is not difficult to output to video formats (DVD, HD, SD) that can be used to show investors or for creative approvals or previews to test versions of the film with theater audiences.

As a side note, there are quite a few companies whose purpose is only to create opening and closing title sequences. Because the filmmaker and the production company are consumed with preparing the film, the opening titles are often subcontracted to another production company that specializes in opening credit sequences. It is not uncommon for the title company to shoot additional footage for the opening of the film. The incorporation of new graphics that relate to the film itself is a part of the opening title creation. More often than not, the opening titles are delivered as files to the DI company and integrated into the final film.

Continuing on with the film digital intermediate process, once the footage is loaded, the images can be manipulated. Like most computer processes, the original digitizing or transfer process is time consuming, but once the images are loaded, color correction, dirt removal, and even some effects work (depending on which computer program is used) are possible. This is why so many feature films are now using this process. Not only does the DI process allow for a great degree of control over the image, the image can also be projected and screened, and then changes can be made.

For video professionals, this does not seem so radical, because this type of image manipulation is common throughout the post production process. However, the NTSC video frame is incredibly small compared to the large image resolution of a film frame. For film professionals, the ability to store, correct, manipulate, and view changes using large-scale film files of this type is considered revolutionary.

The choice of a DI company does not come lightly. Feature films are often on a tight schedule. More often than not, production and other delays can occur. However, as experienced postproduction crews know, despite production or other delays, delivery dates do not easily change.

Using information from the offline nonlinear editing system, the film files are matched (conformed) to the way the program was edited in the NLE. Effects are incorporated, color is corrected, opening and closing titles are created or incorporated, and the final product is then output to film.

Some non-linear editing systems are not capable of tracking film key numbers. Key numbers are exposed numbers on the edge of the film that identify each frame. It is important to know if your offline, creative editing system is capable of outputting at film cut list. Otherwise, the conforming process becomes a manual process. The solution for this type of problem would be if a show was edited on a nonlinear editor using down converted video footage with burn-ins of the key numbers. Then these numbers could be manually written down and used as a source to pull the actual film negative.

LUTs

Original film-scanned files actually look terrible. However, when properly treated and output to film, the results are spectacular. There is an intermediate step in viewing these files. Look-Up Tables (LUTs) are used to translate the digital film files into the images that they will look like when exposed to film. LUTs are a very important part of the DI process.

Not to Be Taken Lightly

Although the concept of DI is fairly straightforward, it is not to be taken lightly, as it is an expensive process. DI can be 23.98 or 24 frames per second. Film runs at 24 frames per second, but out of the telecine, it can also run at 23.98 or 24. NTSC video runs at 29.97; flex files from telecine are used to convert the 23.98 information to 29.97, creating an accurate negative cut list. In order for the DI to work smoothly and correctly, there must be constant communication and equipment checks (CCEC).

The Video Versus Film Gap

There has been a gap between video and film professionals for years. Because film has traditionally had a much higher quality image, requiring very demanding effects and lab work, film technicians and workers have looked down on the electronic or video process. Part of the reason that this gap existed is that the filmmakers believed their works, viewed on huge screens, were far more important and critical than the small screen images that video productions represented. This began to change as high definition entered the production world.

With the addition of the DI process, the line between film, electronics, and video started to become blurred. Filmmakers became very cognizant of the limitations of film postproduction and the rapid improvements in electronics from editing programs to digital projection in the theater. Visionaries like George Lucas declared he would not shoot on film ever again. Finally, high definition video brought film and video producers to the same electronic playing field.

Now the video professionals were presented with the same challenges as their film counterparts: mixed media, and crystal clear pictures that revealed image flaws and effect work that would be examined frame by frame. The video professionals were also confronted with the economic realities of dealing with large-scale images.

The video versus film image gap still exists. Film is transferred at 4:4:4, usually at a 10-bit depth. Most video HD productions are shot at 1080i59.97, with color sub sampling at 4:2:2 with an 8-bit depth. That is a huge difference, both in computer file size and cost of manipulation, but high definition video can also be recorded at 1080p24, 4:4:4 (no chroma subsampling), and in 10-bit depth. With all of this added data, this progressive high definition image can make an excellent DI file.

- A friend of mine went to a multiplex and watched a movie, then struck out to see the digital projection of the same film. She was amazed: "The digital image is so much clearer," she came away saying. A little more investigation revealed that there are some 50 to 100 flagship theaters in the country that get special treatment through the DI process. Normally, the DI output is exposed to negative film, which in turn creates an interpositive, and then an internegative. This last film, the internegative, is the source of most of the country's film prints.
- However, the flagship theaters get a different treatment. The DI is output to negative, which is then used to create the flagship prints. This saves two film generations in the laboratory. My suspicion is that my friend first saw one of the non-flagship prints, which had gone through another generation of film duplication and then saw the digital projection, which is basically a color-corrected, compressed file of the original camera negative.

No matter what the origin of the DI file, the output process remains the same. Once the project has been assembled and altered to everyone's satisfaction, it is then exposed or "burned" back onto a film negative. This is an expensive process. Each frame is exposed to a frame of film, and then the film is developed. From this point, traditional lab work takes over and prints are made and distributed.

Film is Not a Good Duplication Medium

It is a well-known fact that film does not hold up well through multiple generations. The digital intermediate process has provided filmmakers with a shortcut from original material to the screen without having to sacrifice visual quality because of film generation degradation.

The great advantage of the DI process is that multiple film negatives can be made from it. There is no generational loss from effects work. High definition filmmakers benefit from HD as well. From HDV to DVCPro HD to HD, filmmakers are shooting at a true 24 frames as well as 23.98, and creating their DV and DVDs to find an audience or a film competition award. If they win the grand prize of economic support or are invited to screen their movie in a larger venue, they can then output to film and release their product theatrically.

In the past 12 months alone, HD cameras, HD recording, and HD mimicking of film depth of field have greatly improved. Now, with more tools and greater latitude and certainly more field experience as well as success with previous projects, HD has definitely moved into feature film production.

The End of Film?

As mentioned in Chapter Two, the days of film are definitely numbered. In the beginning years of video production, film professionals scoffed at the idea that this low resolution medium with little postproduction support could ever grow into a medium that rivaled the high image quality of film.

But electronics move very fast. With the lowered cost of media storage and incredible increases in processing speed, software, and video recording capabilities, high definition video is poised to overtake film entirely. Incredible as it may seem, HD production in the next few years will very likely not only overtake film as a viable production medium, it will also actually make the ATSC DTV table obsolete.

Currently today's NTSC compatible cameras, video tape, and editing systems far exceed the antiquated, fuzzy composite NTSC broadcast delivery system that brings these images into our homes. At the rate HD development is going, it will not take long before HD cameras and recorders surpass the resolution of film. With a few more electronic adjustments to simulate depth of field, camera controls, and film grain, true filmmaking will become a lost art.

There is no doubt: HD is here to stay as a film and broadcast medium that is going to improve rapidly and continue to drop in cost.

Chapter Eight Summary

- High definition has been used as a production medium for more than a few major feature films and its use is growing rapidly.

- Some filmmakers begin the DI process, loading files and starting color correction, but output portions, or the entire unfinished project, to show potential investors. When additional monies are acquired, the DI process can continue at full speed.

- Not only does DI offer multiple, pristine film negatives for creating theatrical prints, it also ensures a "true to the original" high definition as well as standard definition master for ancillary markets.

The film workflow has several possible paths:

- Shoot HD, edit offline, conform HD, enter DI, output film

- Shoot film, edit offline, cut film negative, enter DI, output film

- Shoot film, transfer to HD, edit offline, conform HD, enter DI, output film

- There are a few companies whose purpose is only to create opening and closing title sequences.

- DI is not a toy and is not to be taken lightly.

- Film is not a good duplication medium.

- The End of Film is coming—it's just a matter of when.

CHAPTER 9

Employment Opportunities and New Horizons

From preproduction, to production, and into postproduction, high definition has many opportunities and they are rapidly growing. It is interesting to note that many of the skills required for high definition production are the same ones that were needed for standard definition. Of course, there are added issues in the high def world that require new information and experience, like knowing about camera operation at 24 frames per second versus 23.98 frames per second, or being aware of the framing and compositing issues depending on whether the HD program is going to be down-converted or viewed in standard definition.

In the postproduction world, many additional skills are needed. Knowledge concerning frame rates and the abilities and limitations of nonlinear editors is vital. Someone who knows the current frame rate, recording, and camera possibilities would certainly be a valuable asset to any production company. An acquaintance of this author's makes a good living aligning high definition monitors for HD multiple camera shoots. This type of expertise is unique and in demand. Another acquaintance is a very well-respected cinematographer specializing in high definition production.

Of course, in HD there is still a demand for entry level positions, which run the gamut from production assistants to researchers. Again, the high definition production does not have to be complicated. If frame rates and frame sizes are kept constant (CCEC), the process can be easy and even fun. Remember: delivery format determines the production format.

With cable channels creating their own original programming, international sporting events being viewed in the United States, the huge amount of reality programming being produced, and pay cable creating its own specials and original shows, the employment opportunities that are being offered in high def are growing rapidly. If one is familiar with and knowledgeable about postproduction workflows, one can most likely be employed today if one knows the HD production companies that are looking for high definition experience.

Many companies trying to understand and convert to high definition are in need of help. As it goes beyond the basic knowledge that production companies need to know, there are many people about to be hired to work specifically on high definition productions. Unfortunately, many people think that if they have experience in high definition, they will be employed by these HD companies. This is not always true. The people who are going to be hired are those individuals who have contacts within those production companies.

As mentioned earlier, keeping a contact list is vital to the success of any individual in any business. Even if you plan to be a director or producer, who is going to score your film or design your costumes? As one travels life's path, there will be people that cross it who bring new information. Often, these people may not be offering information that is relevant to the moment. Many times we meet people whose skills or information we will need in the future.

No matter what business you are in or planning to join, an incredible number of people will cross your path who will want to and be able to help you in your career. Keeping a list of these people's names, interests, and contact information will prove invaluable.

On the Horizon

High definition is an electronic medium that will continue to evolve and improve, and these changes will come quickly.

There are frame rates in the ATSC table that do not even have hardware invented for them, and there are frame rates with no existing cameras. But these advanced picture specifications will become available and the 60p format will be exciting in its own right. The most exciting part about this electronic revolution is that editing systems, record decks, codecs, hard drives, computer speed, and even broadcast compression will continue to improve dramatically.

And there is no doubt about two other things as well:

> The high definition confusion will subside and settle into several established production paths and frame rates, most likely progressive integer.
> High definition production, as well as postproduction, will continue to evolve, improve, and make new challenges for all of us.

Future Sales of Today's Productions

During the 1960s, no one had any idea that those television shows would end up filling hours of programming on cable channels. Nowadays, producers, networks, and production companies are careful not to be so shortsighted and to protect their visual products. Even shows that are not intended to be released on high def are being produced in HD def so that, if or when there is a demand for even more visual product, they can deliver not only in high definition but in other formats as well.

High Def Will Be the Norm

High definition and digital broadcasting are here and are rapidly growing in use both professionally and by consumers. Several HDV consumer video cameras are on the market. Not only are people making a living at weddings and birthdays videos using these relatively inexpensive tools, professionals are putting them to use also.

There is no denying that in the coming years high definition will continue grow rapidly as consumers become accustomed to the detailed images that HD brings into their homes. When the analog frequencies are shut off in 2009, there will be millions of high definition sets in use. NTSC will be as old and obsolete as black and white television. High definition will rule the broadcast airwaves and we will again move into new frame rates, those without decimals—full integer frame rates.

High definition has arrived.

CHAPTER 10

Steve Browne's Personal Summary

With every new format, conversion, or dramatic change in technology, there are those who drag their feet, and these are the people who get left behind, complain about the good old days, and do not accept the new order of things. Just as there were individuals who bemoaned the advent of talking pictures, color film, stereo audio, and premium cable channels, some people just do not want to leave the comfort of a 4 × 3 low-quality single frame rate video format. But technology marches on, and that march is becoming faster and faster. Who would have thought that millions of people would actually pay for satellite radio? Those who ignore reality hide their heads in the sand.

High definition is here to stay. With its various frame rates and frame sizes, there is certainly an understandable amount of confusion. Yet in a short amount of time, all of this will pass and we will enter a time of high definition calm.

Hardly anyone even remembers the first handheld calculators that cost over a thousand dollars. Or what about those huge bulky cell phones? Things have definitely changed. Even high definition equipment will drop in price, and HDV and high definition will be the norm. NTSC video will be so passé, those of you reading this book will tell those who follow about the dark years as we made the transition to HD.

HDV Works!

One thing I have been very surprised about is the reliability of HDV. I have onlined several reality shows shot completely in HDV. After reading the specs for MPEG-2 with its GOP (group of pictures) format, I was very skeptical. Yet after seeing, editing, and capturing hours of footage shot in HDV, I have seen few errors due to the MPEG compression. Yes, I converted the HDV to HD on input. This workflow required a lot of media storage, but the result was impressive and the show that aired on HBO looked great.

And finally, Steve Browne's conservative predictions for the future are:

- High definition will become a hot item in consumer purchasing and in production.

- Progressive versus interlaced programming will become a party discussion, with progressive televisions sweeping the county and the interlaced supporters becoming fewer and fewer in numbers.

- Progressive 1080p60 and 1080p24 will not only become the preferred high definition frame rates for directors and producers, but theaters will also start projecting films at these rates as well.

- High definition, coupled with the digital intermediate process, will become so inexpensive, versatile, and high-quality that film will only be used as an acquisition format for projects that want that "old look."

- And lastly, one current and very well-established nonlinear editing system will cease to exist due to the company's resistance to change.

A Few HD Connections

There are quite a few HD connections that are in use. These are several of the more popular ones.

FireWire

FireWire, although technically not an HD connection, has been around for quite a while; FireWire was originally used for DV input and output. With the advent of HDV, the incredible format of HD, and a

Figure A-1 FireWire, developed by Apple computer, is a commonly used way to import and export HDV files.

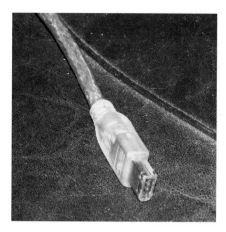

Figure A-2 This D-shaped six-pin FireWire connector is often used to connect external hard drives.

bitrate equal to that of DV, FireWire has now been put into double duty, being used as a DV conduit and an HDV input/output pipeline.

Again, with additional hardware, this FireWire pipeline can be used several ways. One would be to down-convert the HDV signal to standard definition. An HDV image contains much higher resolution than DV, so down-converting HDV to standard definition is often used to replace DV or even other standard camera situations.

Another use of the HDV FireWire portal is to immediately convert the image to HD, as was done for *Dane Cook's Tourgasm* HBO comedy series.

HD-SDI

A common connection within professional wiring systems is a BNC connector at the end of coaxial cable to carry HD-SDI (high definition serial digital interface). This connection provides a nominal data rate of 1.485 Gbits. The advantage of this connection and wiring scheme is that it can be easily and quickly switched to become an SDI signal path if the proper wires are used. However, just because a BNC connector is at the end of a cable does not necessarily mean it can transmit HD-SDI or even SDI. HD-SDI carries digital picture and audio information. However,

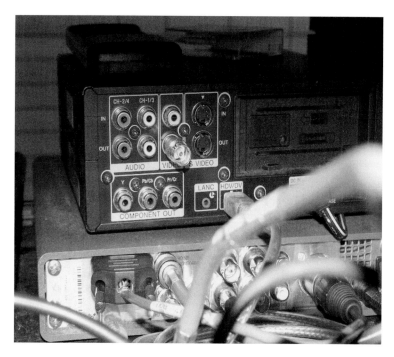

Figure A-3 This picture of a Sony HDV player atop a Miranda converter shows the FireWire connector out of the HDV deck and also the BNC HD-SDI output.

it is only available as professional video equipment due to licensing agreements that restrict the use of unencrypted digital interfaces to professional equipment, and prohibit their use as consumer equipment.

DVI

A digital video interface is often used for DLP, LCD, and plasma displays. Introduced in 1998, it was designed to be used primarily for PC monitoring.

HDMI

A new interface HDMI not only carries video signals, but it also is able to replace up to eight audio cables. This interface is garnering a lot of interest in the home consumer market.

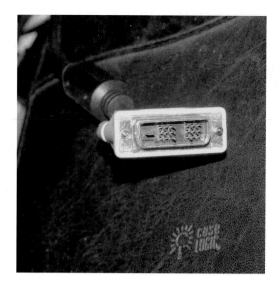

Figure A-4 This digital-only connector is a common connector for desktop monitors.

USB 2.0

Able to run up to 480 Mbps and less expensive than the established FireWire connection, USB is a connection choice that is included in current computers. However, the established FireWire connection seems to be used more often than the newer USB 2 connector.

Ethernet

This is another common connection, especially for home use. With speeds up to 1 Gbps available now, it is starting to be used more often to transport data, including digital audio and video.

Glossary

¾-inch offline—a ¾-inch videotape that is output from an offline edit system, which is used as a reference for a show that is to be onlined. (See also three-quarter inch tape.)

1920 by 1080 pixels—the number of pixels in the high definition 1080 frame. The ratio is 1920 horizontal pixels by 1080 vertical pixels.

1:33—the original film ratio, which was adopted as the NTSC standard (4 × 3).

1:66—a common film ratio of 5×3, sometimes expressed as "1.67."

1:77—a common film ratio where the image is in a 16 × 9 ratio. This is also the ratio of high definition video broadcasting.

1:85—a common film ratio, also referred to as "flat."

10-bit—a digital recording method where 10 bits of digital information are recorded for each of the three components of an image. 10-bit recording supplies enough information for over 1000 possible colors. Most feature films utilizing video recording or scanning create video data at the 10-bit level.

10-bit color depth—indicates that the videotape is recording a signal of 10 bits for each of the three components of a video. 10-bit color that records enough data so that 1024 colors can be displayed.

1080 by 1920—one of the two high definition frame sizes as defined by 1080 vertical lines (of pixels) by 1920 horizontal pixels. Even though other formats like HDV have 1080 vertical pixels, they do not have 1920 horizontal pixels.

1080i29.97—see 1080i 59.94.

1080i59.94—one of the 12 high definition formats defined by the ATSC digital broadcast Table 3. It is also known as 1080 59.94i, 59.94i, and 1080i 29.97. This format contains 1080 vertical pixels.

It is the broadcast format chosen by CBS, NBC, and almost all the HD cable channels.

1080psf23.98—considered a high definition "universal format." This size and frame rate can be converted with few complications to the other formats by reducing the frame size, altering the playback speed, or introducing 3:2 pulldown.

16 millimeter film—a film format that was used for many purposes, including early filmmaking and much of the early television news footage. Various videotape formats have replaced 16 millimeter.

16 × 9 format—the horizontal and vertical ratios for high definition television. It is also another expression for the 1.77 film format.

2:3 pulldown—a film transfer process where the film frame is first transferred to two video fields, then the next film frame is transferred to three video fields. The process is repeated, and the extra field with every other frame ends up creating six extra frames per second. These six frames of added visual information are the exact amount required to make a 24-frame film series of images into a 30-frame video. It is important to note that when this transfer occurs, most of the time the film rate is slowed down by 1% in order to keep sync with NTSC and high definition decimal frame rates. The high def decimal frame rates are specifically designed to be compatible with NTSC. 2:3 pulldown is also called 3:2 pulldown.

2:35—a common film ratio accomplished either of two ways: through the use of anamorphic lenses, the result of which is a 2:35 image when unsqueezed; or when a movie is shot on super 35, exposing the entire aperture, including the area where the sound track would reside, and then a center extraction is made and the image is stretched vertically or squeezed horizontally, the result of which is a 2:35 format.

23.98 frames per second is not always 24 frames per second—it is important to note that many sales brochures and other information identify HD and HDV camera rates as 24 frames per second. Often this can actually mean 23.98. On the other hand, 24 frames per second can really mean 24 frames per second. Many camera manuals are available online, and it is a good idea to check a camera's frame rate capabilities.

24 frames per second—the rate that film is shot during "normal" film production. It is also referred to as "sound speed" because film can be exposed at different frame rates to achieve desired effects like slow motion. Some video cameras and editing systems mistakenly identify 24 frames per second when in reality the frame rate is 23.98.

29.97 is not 30 but is not necessarily 59.94i—amid all the confusion about frame rates, it is important to know that 29.97 can be recorded in both progressive and interlaced recording, and that there are two integer high definition frame rates of 30 frames per second, one progressive and one interlaced.

29.97 standard definition—this is essentially the ATSC's version of NTSC video. However, it is different from the original NTSC signal because ATSC's digital signal is 720 by 480 (the same as the NTSC DV format), rather than the 720 by 486 lines used in NTSC production and broadcasting.

2K—the name for a film scan, creating a 2048 × 1556 pixel image for each film frame.

30 frames per second—often refers to 29.97 frames per second. True 30 frames per second is rarely used.

35 millimeter film—the film industry standard on which most feature films are shot. This 4 × 3 ratio image is very impressive and has been the mainstay of film production and projection for over 60 years. Recently, high definition video and separately, the digital intermediate process, have made inroads into the feature film production work path. In addition, digital projectors in theaters have been installed. Over the last few years, the dominance of 35mm lab work has been threatened by the digital intermediate. Ultimately, film will be pushed aside in theatrical production and projection, becoming another obsolete technology.

4 × 3—a common film and video ratio. Also expressed as 1:33. Also, the original ratio of film production as well as projection. The United States' original format, NTSC video, was a 4 × 3 ratio. This is still the ratio of 35 millimeter film (however, the image is matted for theatrical exhibition). The ratio of high definition video is 16 × 9 (16 units wide by 9 units tall).

4,096 pixels—the number of pixels in film frames' full aperture 4K scan from film to computer data.

4:1:1—a way to indicate a pattern of a color subsampling rate. This rate basically samples one color pixel for every four luminance pixels. Or to put it differently; for every luminance pixel, the color is sampled only 25% of the time. The human brain does not decipher color as well as black and white. Thus, visually, color information is less critical than black and white information.

4:2:0—a way to indicate a pattern of a color subsampling rate. The luminance is sampled every line, but the chroma is not sampled on the first line, 4:0:0, but then is sampled on the next one (4:2:2).

4:2:2—a way to indicate a pattern of a color sampling rate, it indicates where the sampling frequency of the chroma is half that of the luminance value. Currently considered a de facto standard for high definition broadcast recording, this sampling rate is seen as inadequate for major feature film acquisition. However, some HD productions using this subsampling rate have also been used for film productions.

4:4:4—a way to indicate a pattern of a color sampling rate. This indicates where the sampling rate of the chroma values is equal to that of the luminance values.

45 Mb/s—the bandwidth limitation of Ku-band satellites. These satellites are used to distribute signals to the network affiliate stations and cable companies.

4K—This refers to a film transfer to data resulting in a file size of 4096 pixels horizontally and 3112 pixels vertically. 4K is a very expensive process. Its purpose is to capture the most image information to allow the highest quality of digital manipulation.

4K scan—a large data file created by scanning a frame of film and transferring the image into a data file containing 4096 pixels.

59.94i—see 1080i59.94.

720 and 1080—the two vertical frame sizes defined by the ATSC as high definition frame sizes.

720p—the vertical resolution of the HD highly regarded Panasonic VariCam. This HD size can be "uprezed" to the often required 1080 high definition. This is also one of the vertical pixel resolutions defined by the ATSC Table 3 of digital television (DTV).

720p50.94—a progressive HD size and frame rate used by ABC and ESPN as a standard.

8-bit color depth—an 8-bit depth means there are 8 bits of information for each of the three values that describe a pixel, or 24 bits per pixel. An 8-bit depth allows 256 colors to be displayed at one time. 10-bit is the next step up in color depth.

AAF—see Advanced Authoring Format.

ABC—the American Broadcasting Network. This company, owned by the Walt Disney Company, broadcasts its high definition programs at 720p59.94.

Adobe—a major software manufacturer that makes editing, DVD burning, audio, video compositing, photo manipulation, and other software. Adobe has created several powerful visual programs: Photoshop for the manipulation of still pictures; Aftereffects for the creation of visual effects; and Premiere Pro, an editing program.

Adrenaline—a brand of video editing system that is manufactured by Avid, a leading digital video, audio, and data storage company.

Advanced Authoring Format—a file format designed to transfer Avid sequence information to other nonlinear editing systems.

Advertisers—a loose term describing companies that purchase commercial time in a variety of venues. As a general rule, advertisers are some of the first users of innovative video productions and effects. Advertisers were slow to accept high definition as they felt too few people were watching and the production cost was too high.

After Effects—a popular effects program from Adobe software. This program works by importing images, manipulating them, and then outputting the results in a variety of different formats.

Analog—a method of recoding information by modulating the information onto a carrier wave. The major alternative to this method would be sampling and recording data information in a digital form. (See digital.)

Analog NTSC frequencies—the original frequencies assigned by the Federal Communications Commission (FCC) to each television station in the country. New digital frequencies were assigned to each station for the new DTV standards. The old analog frequencies will be returned to the government in 2009.

Apple—an innovative computer company that has not only created a very powerful line of computers, but also a series of popular video software. These products include Final Cut Pro, Motion Soundtrack, Motion, DVD Studio, and Shake.

Apple Motion—a popular effects program created by Apple Computer Corporation.

Apple Shake—a compositing program created by Apple Computer Corporation.

Approval—a term indicating that the person or persons in charge have seen a visual program and have signed off on it. Usually, the more expensive the program, the more people are required to give their approval.

Approval dubs—copies of an offline or finished product in a format that a client can view. The format may vary and can include (but not limited to) VHS, mini DV, and DVD.

ASPECT HD—a program that introduces an intermediate codec for HDV editing in a nonlinear editing system. A third-party software program that is capable of extrapolating flagged video frames from specific cameras that record at 29.97 frames per second and then creating 24 frames per second images.

ATSC—an acronym for the Advanced Television Systems Committee. This organization was formed in 1982 to establish standards for the technical aspects of advanced television systems. It created the famed ATSC Table 3, as well as many other high definition broadcasting specifications.

ATSC digital television table—a table describing the 36 digital television formats. Also known as ATSC Table 3.

Avid—a major manufacturer of digital storage and nonlinear editing systems.

Avid—a series of powerful editing systems, from smaller software-based editing programs to major high-end, high definition systems.

Avid Composer Adrenaline HD—a high definition editing system manufactured by Avid, a leading digital video, audio, and data storage company.

Avid DS—a brand of video editing system manufactured by Avid, a leading digital video, audio, and data storage company. Also called Avid DS or Nitris DS. This is a different computer program from the Symphony Nitris, but utilizes the same hardware.

Avid Symphony Nitris—a high definition editing system manufactured by Avid which utilizes their Nitris hardware. This is a different program from Avid Nitris DS, but uses the same hardware.

Avid Unity Media Network—a shared network of drives manufactured by Avid that can be used by many different workstations.

BetaMax—an old NTSC home video format that was manufactured by the Sony Corporation. The competing format, VHS, eventually won the battle.

Beta SP—an improvement over the original Sony BetaCam format.

Bit depth—a designation as to how many colors a digital file contains. (See 8-bit color depth, 10-bit.)

Bitmap—a Windows graphics file format.

Blue screen—the process of recording an image in front of a blue background. The intent is to remove the blue from the image through the use of an effect and replace that color with a different image. Green also can be used for the background. The choice of blue or green depends on the colors of the foreground object being photographed. (See Green screen.)

Blurring—the act of visually removing logos, faces, or artwork that have not been legally cleared to be included in a program.

Broadcast quality—a subjective description of a visual image that is judged as having adequate clarity to be aired on television. There really is no technical description of broadcast quality. As video recording techniques and equipment have improved, so has the expectation of a video picture.

Broadcasters—a generic term for companies and individuals working in the field of transmitting radio and television signals.

Budget considerations—the economic constraints that are put on a project.

Burn-in—the imprinting of a video signal with text, numbers, and symbols. This information varies with original film information, show running times, production information, and even copyright information.

Cable channel—a video transmission over a cable company's delivery system. This channel could have been originally broadcast over the airwaves and then sent down the cable, or received via satellite from a cable-only broadcaster.

Cable company—a company whose primary purpose is to receive video and audio signals from a variety of sources and deliver them to a consumer's home via a physical cable. The sources a cable company could provide include, but are not limited to: local over-the-air stations; premium cable producers like HBO, Showtime, HDNet, DiscoveryHD, and so forth; or other programming choices such as music, on-demand programming, and local government access.

Canopus—brand name of a popular digital editing program.

Cathode ray tube (CRT)—a large vacuum tube that is used in oscilloscopes, monitors, and televisions to display images. A cathode ray shoots out of an emitter; through the use of high voltage deflection coils, this ray is guided across the face of a coated tube, causing the phosphors on the face of the tube to glow. Until LCD, DLP, and plasma screens came along, this was the mainstay of visual technology. It is becoming an obsolete technology.

CBS—an acronym for Columbia Broadcasting System, one of the largest television networks in the United States.

CCEC—stands for "constant communication and equipment check," two vital processes that should be done throughout the production of a program.

CGI—a "computer-generated image." This usually refers to an effect or background image, whether moving or still.

Cinepak—a popular and effective picture and audio compression codec.

Clip—a portion of a scene or take.

Clone—an exact copy of a digital tape or file. There is no difference or loss if a clone is created properly.

Closed captioning—the process of transcribing, then encoding the text of a video program onto a specific vertical line of the program. The show is transcribed, then through the use of specialized equipment, this text information is digitally inserted into the program. Many televisions and monitors have decoding equipment that interprets and then displays this text. In some instances, closed captioning is inserted into live programming.

Codec—a process where a digital file is mathematically reduced in size, yet the integrity of the file is maintained. The word comes from a shortening of the words "code/decode." In terms of video codecs, some are recording codecs employed by the video recording deck. Others are input codecs used by digital editing systems, and still others are output codecs used for delivery. Some codecs work better than others for their specific purpose.

Color correction—the process of altering the original color of a video shot. There are several reasons one might color correct a shot. These include fixing a problem that occurred in the recording process, evening color differences between cameras, evening out lighting differences between shots, or perhaps to give a scene or program a specific look or a certain "feel" to elicit an emotional response.

Color sampling—the amount of recording of chroma information in comparison to the amount of luminance recorded. Since human vision recognizes black and white more readily than color, color is often sampled (recorded) less than luminance in order to save space on tape or computer drives. The color sampling is usually expressed in the form of X:X:X where the first X represents the luminance sampling and the next two numbers indicate the chroma sampling. (See 4:4:4, 4:2:2, 4:2:0.)

Color subsampling—The process of recording less color information in comparison to the recording of the luminance portion of
the signal.

Colorists—individuals who color film or video using color correction equipment. Colorists often are involved in the transfer of
film images to videotape.

Combustion—a compositing program from the Discrete company,
a major manufacturer of digital editing, effects, and compositing
programs.

Component—video designed to have three separate parts: luminance, designated by the symbol Y; a chroma value that represents Y (luminance) subtracted from the color red, represented by
the symbol R-Y; and a third number that is the Y (luminance) subtracted from the color blue, represented by the symbol B-Y. The
color green is derived through a mathematical equation using
these three values.

Component video—the video recording process of recording the
three values (y, r-y, b-y) of a video signal. This process requires
three wires to transmit its image. Previously, video was recorded
in a composite manner, with the three components stored and
transmitted as a single signal.

Composite—the video process of recording, displaying, or transmitting a color video signal that requires one wire to transmit
its signal. This is how NTSC signals are broadcast and how they
were recorded for many years. Advancement in electronic equipment allowed the introduction of digital composite recording,
and eventually digital component recording.

Compression—a way of taking a digital signal of 1's and 0's and,
through a complex formula, encoding it so that much of the
information is still present, but in a smaller form. Color sampling of luminance and chrominance is one form of compression.
Compression almost always happens either in the camcorder or
the camera's outboard video recorder. The next time compression
occurs is on the input to the nonlinear computer editor. Several
high-end editing systems edit 1:1, which means that there is no
compression on input even though the original signal may have
been compressed at the video recorder. Compression is considered necessary because a high definition frame occupies a huge
amount of computer storage space.

Consumer flatscreen—LCD, plasma, or DLP displays are considered consumer flatscreens. Usually the difference between a

professional and consumer display is that a professional model can be finely tuned and calibrated. Consumer models have general settings and are not very flexible. In addition, the resolution of a consumer model is much lower than that of a professional monitor. Most professionals still use CRT (cathode ray tube) monitors for HD work. (See CRT.)

Consumer format—consumer video formats usually have less ability to record high quality images. VHS and BetaMax were two of the first consumer video formats. The middle ground is called "prosumer," a cross between professional and consumer. These formats, when used carefully, produce a very good image. HDV is considered a prosumer format but is also used in some professional productions.

Contact list—a list of people one has met or needs to meet, their phone numbers and/or addresses. The contact list is used for assembling crews and getting employment, as well as obtaining information. A contact list is an important tool for anyone considering working in the film and video industry.

Continuity—the process of making sure all the elements in a scene remain the same over a series of shots, even if the shots are taken on different days or even in different locations. Continuity takes into account actors' clothes, their placement, background actors, lighting conditions, and so forth.

Crane—a balanced camera mount specially designed to raise, lower, and swing a camera to facilitate moving shots.

Credit block—a listing of the people involved in the making of a movie, placed at the end of a movie commercial.

Credit roll—a moving list of the people involved in the making of a video or film project, usually at the end of a program.

Cut negative—film that was originally exposed during production and has been physically cut. Usually film negative is cut in order to prepare a program for final processing, either in a digital intermediate process, or a traditional film laboratory finish.

D2—a digital composite video format.

D5—a digital component video recorder manufactured by Panasonic. D5 uses a 4:1 compression at 8-bit color depth and 5:1 at 10-bit color depth.

DA88—an 8-track digital audio recorder that can record 1 hour and 48 minutes of program.

DaVinci 2K—brand name of a color correction system.

DDR—a digital disk recorder, which is a device that stores video or other digital data. Two uses of DDRs are for color correction and for effects work, allowing quick and immediate access to digital files.

December 24, 1996—the date that the Federal Communications Commission (FCC) formerly adopted the ATSC Digital Television (DTV) Standards.

Digi Beta—nickname of Sony's Digital BetaCam record or playback deck or tape.

Digital—a process of storing information in a series of 1's and 0's. Digital information can be stored on variety of media, including but not limited to audio tape, videotape, computer chips, optical disks, and hard disks.

Digital BetaCam—Sony's half-inch digital component system, a common broadcast format that compresses video in a 4:2:2 compression space at 10-bit YUV 4:2:2 sampling in PAL (720×576) or NTSC (720×480) resolutions that "flow" through the pipe/wire at a bitrate of 90 Mbit/second.

Digital intermediate (DI) process—a workflow process where either film or high definition video is scanned into a computer, manipulated (color corrected, effected, edited), and then output to film negative. Most often the film negative is used to create film prints for the purpose of projection in a theater.

Director—the "captain" of a film or video project. In film production, the director's job is to make sure the project is completed from beginning to end. Often in episodic broadcast production, the director is only responsible for shooting the episode, and the producer and/or production staff maintains the production schedule while the director prepares to direct the next episode.

Director's cut—the first cut of a film or visual program that includes all the scenes that were shot. This cut is usually very long and includes scenes that do not work or will not end up in the final editing program. This cut of the film is often used as a source for promotional materials. As the show is shown to test audiences, executives, and others, scenes are often dropped, rearranged, and reedited until the best possible show is created.

DirectTV—one of two main premium television satellite delivery companies in the United States, delivering sports, entertainment, and information to consumers' homes via satellite-to-receiver technology. DirectTV is mainly a delivery company and is not responsible for producing very much of its content. The main competitor to DirectTV is DISH Network.

Discovery HD—a premium cable channel that produces high definition documentaries and information programs for satellite and cable delivery to consumers' homes.

Discrete—a high end effects and editing company that manufactures a series of products using their own proprietary hardware.

DISH Network—one of two main premium television satellite delivery companies in the United States, delivering sports, entertainment, and information to consumers' homes via satellite-to-receiver technology. DISH is mainly a delivery company and is not responsible for producing very much of its content. DirectTV is DISH's main competitor.

DLP—one of three flat screen formats. This screen is based on Texas Instruments' proprietary chip. This chip has thousands of mirrors that move, which alters how much light on any color reaches the screen.

DNxHD—a high definition video codec from Avid Technology, a leading video editing and storage provider. This codec has been adapted by several HD production companies because it is specially designed for video postproduction. It is specifically designed to preserve a high level of video imagery while shrinking the size of the data file. Several large broadcast companies have adopted this codec as a standard within their postproduction workflow.

Dolby 5.1—a surround sound format from the Dolby Corporation featuring five channels of audio (front left, front right, front center, back left, and back right) as well as a subwoofer channel.

Dolly—a platform with wheels specially designed to have a camera mounted on it to facilitate moving shots.

Down-conversion—the process of dubbing or converting from a high resolution to one of lesser quality.

Drop frame time code—time code that employs a method of counting video frames that takes into account the difference between 30 frames per second and NTSC's 29.97 frames per second. Drop frame time code is time accurate. Non-drop frame time code is not.

Dropped frames—this occurs when the data path is not capable of handling the data that is being fed down the path. Another cause of dropped frames is when an editing system cannot process a series of effects fast enough to display the final product in real time. In either case, because the frames cannot be processed, they are dropped. Dropped frames are not related to drop frame or non-drop frame time codes.

DTV—digital television, usually meaning over-the-air broadcasting. A signal sent over the airwaves intended to be receieved by an antenna, decoded and then displayed on a television.

Dub—to make a copy of a program. Usually "dub" indicates a copy of an analog program where "clone" would be a digital copy of a digital program through a digital path.

DV—a digital NTSC prosumer video format. Sony took the same format and used it to record on their digital 8 format.

DV Express—a brand of video editing system manufactured by Avid, a leading digital video, audio, and data storage company.

DVCPRO HD—a Panasonic recording and digitizing codec. When employed by a D5 recording, DVCPRO-HD uses 6.7:1 compression and supports 10-bit input and output per channel.

Edit bay—a room where visual editing takes place.

Editor—can either refer to a person who uses an editing machine, or a machine or computer program that edits.

EDL—acronym for Edit Decision List. An edit listing program originally designed for use in linear editing systems to export and import a limited amount of data.

Enhanced definition signals (ED)—the middle range of digital broadcasting formats defined by the ATSC DTV table.

eQ—a Quantel online system that works on a priority software and hardware platform.

ESPN—an acronym for Entertainment Sports Programming Network. This company, owned by the Walt Disney Company, broadcasts its high definition programs at 720p54.94.

Feature film—a film that is shot, usually on film and at least an hour and a half in length, intended for projection and viewing in a theater.

Feature film production—the process of making a film designed to be released theatrically. Can also mean the production phase of a feature film. This phase is often called principal photography. It is during this part of creating a motion picture that the majority of the images are shot either on film or on high definition video. Sometimes a feature film is shot using a camera that sends a data stream rather than a video signal. This data stream is then used to create film files. Other phases are preproduction and postproduction.

Federal Communications Commission (FCC)—the governmental agency that oversees, among other things, radio and television broadcasting in the United States.

Field—one half of a frame in an interlaced video format. There are no fields in a progressive video recording or display.

Film acquisition—the shooting of visual images on film.

Film lab—a company that specializes in the processing of film products.

Film negative—film designed for film acquisition or digital output.

Film output—the process of exposing film from a video source. A film recorder is a very expensive device.

Film studio—a company that finances, oversees, and sometimes distributes film productions, usually in theaters, but it may also use DVDs and home video as distribution venues.

Final Cut Pro—a popular video editing program created by the Apple Corporation.

Fire—brand name of a standard definition and high definition compositing station that has some editing capabilities, manufactured by Autodesk.

FireWire—a very fast standard that supports data transfer rates of up to 400Mbps. Apple originally developed this technology and uses the trademarked name "FireWire." Other companies use other names, such as i.link and Lynx, to describe their 1394 products. Like USB, 1394 supports both plug-and-play and hot plugging, and also provides power to peripheral devices.

Flame—brand name of an Autodesk visual effects design and compositing system.

Frame rate—refers to either the rate at which a program is edited or the rate at which a take is shot. The rate at which frames are either recorded or displayed per second.

Frame size—the horizontal and vertical pixel sizes of a video frame.

FTP—short for file transfer protocol, the protocol for exchanging files over the Internet. FTP uses the Internet's TCP/IP protocols to enable data transfer. FTP is most commonly used to download a file from a server using the Internet or to upload a file to a server.

GOP—acronym for group of pictures. (See group of pictures.)

Green screen—the process of recording an image in front of a green background. The intent is to remove the blue from the image through the use of an effect and replace that color with a different image. Blue also can be used for the background. The choice of blue or green depends on the colors of the foreground object being photographed. (See blue screen.)

Group of Pictures—an MPEG compression technology in which the first frame is recorded, and then the differences of the other frames are recorded. The entire group from the first full frame to the last recorded difference is called a group of pictures. Common groups in MPEG-2 are 15 and 6.

Hardware acceleration—in an editing system, a computer board or entire electronic box, designed specifically to enhance the performance of the editing system.

HBO—acronym for Home Box Office, a premium cable television network that airs theatrically-released feature films, proprietary original full-length television movies, and various original series.

HD ready—a television that is able to display a high definition signal, but does not have a tuner to receive digital over-the-air broadcasts.

HDCAM—one of Sony's high definition recorders. After developing the HDCAM, Sony improved the format with their HDCAM SR (superior recording).

HDCAM SR—an improvement on Sony's HDCAM video recorder. HDCAM SR (superior recording) in 1080i59.94 uses a 10-bit recording format with 4:2:2, recording the compression ratio 2.7:1 in 4:4:4 recording the compression ratio is 4.2:1. In standard quality recording, HD in 4:4:4 "flows" at the rate of 440 Mbps, larger than can be provided with a FireWire connection.

HDNet—a satellite channel that specializes in HD programming.

HDV—MPEG2 compressed high definition signal at 1080i59.94, and its 4:2:0 color subsampling "flows" at 25Mbps, perfect for a FireWire connection.

High def—see high definition.

High definition—720 or 1080 vertical line video signal. High definition has many production formats, but as defined by the ATSC, it has 36 broadcast formats.

High definition data stream—1.485 Gigabits per second. There are very few recorders that can even store this amount of uncompressed high definition video information.

High definition short—a program, usually with a running time of less than an hour, more often less than 40 minutes, shot in high definition. Many times these shorts are used as "calling cards," or as a sample of a filmmaker's work.

IEEE 1394—see FireWire.

Independent filmmaker—a filmmaker who is not tied to a studio or company and raises his or her own funds in order to keep control of the project.

Inferno—a high resolution compositing workstation from Autodesk, designed to work with feature film and high definition images, that also has editing capabilities.

Infinity camera—Grass Valley Company, a subsidiary of the Thompson Group, has their own non-tape camera solution with their Infinity camera, which can record its image to an Iomega cartridge, a FireWire drive, Compact Flash card, or even a USB stick.

iQ—brand name of one of Quantel's high-end editing systems.

Isis—brand name for Avid's powerful shared-storage system.

Isis Media Network—a shared network of drives manufactured by Avid that can be used by many different workstations and is designed for high definition as well as standard definition media files.

LCD—Liquid crystal display, a method of visual display, is created through the use of three liquid crystal cells. In front of these cells is a red, green, or blue filter. Light, which is shone from behind, passes through these filtered cells. The filter is responsible for creating the colors on the screen. The back light is why it has a little more trouble reaching dark blacks.

Leitch Velocity—brand name of a nonlinear editing system.

Letterboxed—the projecting of an image with black masks or mattes at the top and bottom of the screen. A 16 × 9 image in high definition is not letterboxed, but when viewed on a 4 × 3 monitor, in order to see the entire image, the frame is "letterboxed" with mattes at the top and bottom of the frame.

Lighting—one of the important aspects of video and film production. Lighting is probably the most defining portion of a visual production, second only to frames per second.

Linear online editing—a video term referring to the tape-to-tape editing process, usually through a device called a switcher. A switcher is an electronic device that is used to "mix" different sources of video into a single image.

Liquid—a brand of video editing system manufactured by Avid, a leading digital video, audio, and data storage company. This editing system was originally part of a company called Pinnacle, which Avid acquired, and then improved the system.

Lower thirds—the visual identification of a person or place in a visual project. This identification is usually placed in the lower third of the frame.

Matrox—a Canadian company that has created a series of hardware that works within Adobe's editing program called Premiere Pro, to augment the program's capabilities.

Matte—the masking of the top and bottom of a film or video image to create a widescreen experience. Also, a high contrast image that "holds out" or masks a portion of an image to allow another image of the same shape to be inserted into that original picture.

Mbps—stands for millions of BITS per second or megabits per second. It is a measure of bandwidth, the total information flow over a given time.

Media Composer Adrenaline HD—brand name for a nonlinear editing system manufactured by Avid.

MII—a Panasonic half-inch component digital videotape format, which competed with Sony's Digital BetaCam.

Miranda—a device that converts an HDV signal into HD. It is not a playback deck, which is a separate device.

MOS—an acronym that came about in the early days of sound films. Most of the directors were of German descent, and it was common to hear "Mit out Sound" on the set. MOS became the shorthand indication that a shot was to be shot without sync sound.

MPEG—acronym for Moving Picture Experts Group, the nickname given to a family of international standards used for coding audio-visual information in a digital compressed format. The MPEG family of standards includes MPEG-1, MPEG-2, and MPEG-4, formally known as ISO/IEC-11172, ISO/IEC-13818, and ISO/IEC-14496, respectively.

MPEG-2—a compression scheme devised by the Moving Picture Experts Group, a subset of which is used in HD over-the-air digital broadcasting and HDV recording.

MPEG-4—a compression scheme that is twice as efficient as MPEG-2, and one that is being rapidly adopted.

National Television Standards Committee (NTSC)—the group that originally established the television standards for the United States.

NBC—acronym for the National Broadcasting Company, one of the first major television networks.

Negative assembly—the process of pulling a film negative and conforming the original camera footage into a group of film reels.

This conformed negative, spliced together with film cement, is used to make internegatives of the program. Internegatives are then used to create film prints for viewing in theaters.

Network—a company that provides programming to a series of television or cable stations.

New Wave Entertainment—an integrated production and postproduction company. One of its focuses is on motion picture development, implementation, and promotion. New Wave Entertainment is based in Burbank, California.

Nitris DS—a brand of video editing system that is manufactured by Avid, a leading digital video, audio, and data storage company. This is a different computer program from the Symphony Nitris, but it utilizes the same hardware.

Non-drop time code—the time code designed for 59.94i and NTSC (29.97) that counts each frame in a time format, but because the frame rate is 1% less than 30 frames per second, non-drop time code is not time accurate.

NTSC—a composite analog broadcast format that was devised in the forties and fifties for the United States.

October 24, 2005—the date that the United States Senate panel approved the phasing out of analog television broadcast, to occur on April 7, 2009.

Offline/Online edit system compatibility—the ability to effectively transfer a sequence from an offline edit system to an online system. Sometimes this process is unnecessary, as the online conform is done on the same machine as the creative process.

OTA—acronym for over the air. This is generally a description of a broadcast signal from a broadcast tower, as opposed to being received via cable or satellite transmission. An over-the-air signal from a local station could well have been a satellite transmission from another source.

P2 flash media card—a solid state memory card designed to be used in the Panasonic AG-DVX 200 to store images and sound.

Panasonic AG-DVX 200—a camera that is designed to store media and sound on solid state media, and is capable of recording HD using the DVCPRO HD codec.

Photoshop—a widely used program for still image manipulation, which is a product of Adobe.

Pickups—shots that are made after the planned scene or even after completion of principal photography.

Plasma display—a display format that uses a matrix of tiny gas plasma cells to create an image.

Postproduction—the manipulation of images and sound following the production phase of a program.

Postproduction workflow—a predetermined path through which images and sound travel in order to avoid conflicts or potential technological issues.

Premiere Pro—a nonlinear editing system manufactured by Adobe, designed to be used on the IBM/windows computer platform.

Preproduction—the process of preparing for the expensive and intense production phase of a visual program, this includes but is not limited to the following: casting, hiring crew, previsualization, writing, script breakdown, location scouting, and legal preparation, scheduling, and raising production funds.

Previsualization—the process of translating a script into drawn frames for each shot planned during production. Originally called storyboarding because artists drew the frames, now software is often used to perform the previs (previsualization) chores.

Primatte Keyer—a brand name of a very powerful and popular keying software.

Producer—there are several definitions for this term, depending on which kind of production is being undertaken. In television, this is often a writer. In feature filmmaking, it can be the individual who raises the funds, options the script, or is actually overseeing the details of the production. In other types of productions like commercials or DVD-added content, the producer is the middle person between the movie studio or production executive and editors who are cutting the piece.

Production—the process of filming or recording a scripted or live show.

Production company—a company whose primary purpose is to create and deliver a visual or audio program.

Progressive recording—the process of recording or displaying a frame in its entirety. The alternative to progressive recording is interlaced recording.

Prosumer—a term indicating a person or piece of equipment that is midway between a professional and a consumer. An example of a prosumer production would be a wedding or special event shot and edited by a professional. Many HVD cameras are considered prosumer models.

Prosumer format—a cross between a professional and a consumer video recording format. These formats, when used carefully, produce a very good image. HDV is considered a prosumer format.

Proxy file—a second, lower resolution video file with the same images, time code, and audio as the original file that is used for quick transfer and creative editing.

Quad—nickname for the first videotape machine that used two-inch wide videotape and had four (quad) record heads.

Quality control—the process of examining a program for flaws like analog or digital hits, film dirt or hair, or excessive video and chroma levels.

Quantel—a high-end effect and editing company that manufactures a series of products using their own proprietary hardware.

QuickTime—Apple's technology for handling video, sound, animation, graphics, text, and music. Designed to be a flexible platform for creating digital media while maintaining backward compatibility with previous versions.

Safe title—in NTSC video, the portion of the screen that all viewers will be able to see. This is generally considered the inside 80% of the screen. Because many NTSC televisions had different and sometimes poor scanning, text was put into safe title, insuring that 99% of the viewers could see it.

Sampling—the process of taking a digital "snapshot" of a sound or image. The more snapshots per second, the more accurate the digital replication is.

SD—acronym for "standard definition." Standard definition, according to the ATSC table, has a vertical frame size of 480 lines and either 640 or 704 lines horizontally, and is interlaced. NTSC has a vertical frame size of 486 lines.

Shot list—the order of shots that will be attempted the day of a shoot.

Single system—a system in which the audio of a program is recorded on the same media as the picture. When the audio and picture recording systems are separate, it is called a double system.

Slowed down 1%—the NTSC format was originally designed to have 30 frames per second, but when color was introduced, that frame rate was slowed by 1%.

Smoke—brand name of an Autodesk standard definition video editing system, which also has paint, compositing, and color correction capabilities.

Sony—a major manufacturer of electronics equipment.

Sony Vegas6—a nonlinear video program.

Sony XDCAM HD—an HD camera that records to a disk. It can record at three different bit rates (18/25/35 Mbps). In the spring of 2006, the CBS owned and operated organizations (often referred to as O & O's) adopted the XDCAM HD format.

Standard definition protection framing—the process of framing for a 4 × 3 viewing, even though the actual recording area is 16×9.

Steadicam™—a trademarked device that is designed to be strapped to a cameraperson's body. It is meant to balance the weight of the camera to allow smooth movement as the cameraperson moves with the shot.

Stock—the film or videotape used for image recording.

Symphony Nitris—a high definition editing system manufactured by Avid, which utilizes their Nitris hardware. This is a different program from the Avid Nitris DS, but uses the same hardware.

Tape labeling—a necessary but mundane process of noting every-thing about that particular reel, including but not limited to the following: date, production, recording method, frame size, frame rate, reel number, and cameraperson.

Tape-to-tape editing—antiquated method of video editing that is rarely used today.

Telecine—the process of transferring a film image to video or data, or the machine used in this process.

Teranex—a powerful video frame rate converter.

Textless—a program minus all titles, often recorded with split audio tracks allowing the program to be repurposed in different lengths, or even different languages.

Three-chip camera—a camera with three separate chips (a charged coupled device), one for each of the three colors. A single-chip camera uses only one CCD or chip to derive the image.

Three-quarter-inch tape—(also written as ¾-inch tape) a once com-mon videotape format that is used less and less today. Although many decades old, until the past few years, this was often used as a presentation format or one on which to record an offline mas-ter. Recently, DVDs, QuickTime reference files, and DV tape have taken the place of three-quarter-inch tape.

Throughput—the amount of data that is transferred over a digital connection during a given period.

Tiff—a still picture computer file format.

Time code—the frame numbering process in video. Not all time codes are time accurate.

Time of Day (TOD)—the recording of time code on videotape in which the time code is set to the clock time.

Tracking marks—marks on a performer or background, usually bright white, that provide a focus point that allows computer software to track the movement of the object or person.

Trailer company—a company that specializes in creating motion picture trailers and commercials.

Tuner—a device that receives a signal on a predetermined frequency and then decodes a video or audio signal from the frequency.

Ulead Videostudio—a nonlinear video editing software.

Uncompressed—an image that has not been altered by a codec or other method of eliminating redundant data information.

Unity Media Network—a shared network of drives manufactured by Avid that can be used by many different workstations.

Universal format—1080psf23.98 is referred to as a universal format because it can be converted to other formats relatively easily, often by playing it out of a video recorder.

User bits (UBITS)—user bits allow one to record eight digits of information on a videotape. These digits can be any number or the letters A to F. User bits, if available on a particular format of tape, are often used to identify that particular tape. For instance, the ID could be the date and reel number.

Video village—the cluster of equipment that is used to monitor a video or film shoot.

WM9 (Windows Media9)—Microsoft's name for their streaming video technologies.

X:X:X—the symbols used to indicated the color sampling method of a video signal. The first X indicates the luma value almost always expressed in the number 4. The next two Xs are indicators of the number of times the b-luma and the r-luma values are sampled in relation to the luma.

XDCAM HD proxy files—small files recorded by an XDCAM that match the HD images that are simultaneously recorded by the camera. The proxy files are used for creative editing, thus saving drive space. Then, when the edit is complete, the high resolution files are used to conform the piece.

Xpress Pro HD—a high definition editing system manufactured by Avid. It comes as a software-only system, or with a hardware accelerator called Mojo.

Index